THE DOORS OF HEAVEN

Richard Brooks

D1635868

Christian Focus

© Richard Brooks
ISBN 1 85792 397 9

Published in 1998
by Christian Focus Publications, Geanies House,
Fearn, Ross-shire, IV20 1 TW, Great Britain.

Cover design by Donna Macleod

CONTENTS

PREFACE

'Love', according to the old song, 'is a many-splendoured thing'. Heaven, a world of love of a divine and exquisite nature which is beyond compare, is certainly a many-splendoured place. Bright with God's glory, filled with God's presence, centred upon God's throne, permeated with God's holiness, resounding with God's praise, prepared for God's people – it is, in every way, beyond our present limited capacities to take in.

This book is about heaven. Teaching about heaven is spread throughout the Bible, and, in measure, the present treatment reflects this. However, in order to give a certain unity and compactness to our study, we shall concentrate upon drawing out the main lines of the doctrine of heaven from just one book – the last book – of the Bible, the book of Revelation. A vast wealth of riches is there to be discovered. Each of the following chapters focuses upon one particular aspect of the subject, though, it has to be said, this is no more than just a beginning. I would add that while this volume stands on its own as a separate and specific study, it may also be seen as a companion piece to my commentary on the book of Revelation.[1]

At the conclusion of each chapter is some specially selected material from some of our choice brethren in the faith who have pursued their pilgrim path before us, and have now entered into heaven themselves. Their eyes now see the King in his beauty. These 'great old boys' (if we may so speak of them, with respectful affection) dwelt much upon heaven. These excerpts from their writings are included not only because what they have left for us is so profitable in itself (and, I trust, will be found to be so as you read it), but in the hope that you, my readers, will be encouraged to search out more of their works for yourselves, where much more of the same solid, sweet and spiritual substance can be found.

It was said of the Puritan minister, Richard Sibbes, 'heaven was in him, before he was in heaven'. Oh! that the same could be said of us as well, and that these very modest studies of what is so great and glorious a doctrine would assist to that end. May God grant it so – and to him alone shall be the praise!

1

THE GOD OF HEAVEN

If you are genuinely interested in considering the subject of heaven, you must start with God himself. Let two choice servants of God underscore this for us straightaway. C H Spurgeon remarks: 'The fact is, that heaven is God fully enjoyed', and 'Who knoweth God knoweth heaven'. J C Ryle confirms the same: 'Heaven is unceasing godliness: it is to be in the presence of God and his Christ for evermore. God is the light, the food, the air of heaven. It is an eternal sabbath. To serve God is heaven's employment, to talk with God is heaven's occupation'.

There is much confused and sentimental thinking about heaven. Some, of course, would deny its existence altogether, and would do the same with hell. Many would be very willing to have heaven (if they could), but without God. However, let it be understood at the outset: no God, no heaven!

Two of the most magnificent chapters in the entire book of Revelation are chapters 4 and 5, and this is where we begin. Back in Old Testament times, the prophet Ezekiel recorded that 'the heavens were opened and I saw visions of God' (Ezek. 1:1). Such was the experience also of the apostle John. A fresh vision is given to him at the start of chapter 4. A new vista opens before his eyes. 'After these things I looked, and behold, a door standing open in heaven' (4:1).

Three fundamental features concerning heaven and the

God of heaven stand out as the vision unfolds through these two chapters.

Heaven is God's dwelling place

This is the very first thing – not surprisingly and quite rightly – which strikes John as he peers through this door standing open in heaven. What would you expect to have seen? Surely one sight, and one sight only. 'Immediately I was in the Spirit; and behold, a throne set in heaven, and one sat on the throne' (4:2). He saw a throne – and someone sitting on it. And who is that one? It is none other than God himself, the Lord God, the Almighty, the Most High.

Here is one of several Bible verses which declare that heaven is God's dwelling place. Heaven is not some vague 'somewhere out there'. Heaven is a location where (in a most special sense) God dwells. It is a particular place which (in a most special manner) he has chosen for himself to make his tabernacle, his temple, his habitation, his dwelling.

It is quite true, of course, that God is omnipresent. That is to say, he is present everywhere, and cannot be limited, boxed up or pinned down in any way. '"Do not I fill heaven and earth?" says the LORD' (Jer. 23:24). That fact, however, does not in any way cut across heaven being God's dwelling place, his throne room. Recall two verses from Isaiah. 'For thus says the high and lofty one who inhabits eternity, whose name is holy: "I dwell in the high and holy place"' (57:15). And where is that 'high and holy place' where the 'high and lofty one' dwells? Heaven! Or there is Isaiah's plea to God: 'Look down from heaven, and see from your habitation, holy and glorious' (63:15). And where is God's 'habitation (NIV, lofty throne) holy and glorious' from which

he looks down and beholds the children of men? Heaven!
Then there is that text in Ecclesiastes which recalls, 'For
God is in heaven, and you on earth; therefore let your words
be few' (5:2). Or the psalmist David's stirring treatment of
this same theme in Psalm 139, beginning 'Where can I go
from your Spirit? Or where can I flee from your presence?'
(139:7). And there are the Saviour's own words to his disciples when he was teaching them to pray: 'In this manner,
therefore, pray: Our Father in heaven, hallowed be your
name' (Matt. 6:9).

So while, as king Solomon acknowledged in prayer, 'Behold, heaven and the heaven of heavens cannot contain you'
(1 Kgs. 8:27), he continued in the very same prayer (on the
solemn occasion of the dedication of the temple), 'hear the
supplication of your servant and of your people Israel. When
they pray towards this place, then hear in heaven your dwelling-place; and when you hear, forgive' (8:30).

Heaven, then, is God's dwelling place. It is where his
throne is. It is where (in the language of Scripture) he is
seated upon his throne. He is the one 'who sits in the heavens' (Ps. 2:4). To have any other or lesser view of heaven
than that is to be way off the mark. Think of heaven, and
you must think of God. Think of going to heaven, and you
must think of going to be with God. Think of getting to
heaven, and you must think first of getting right with God.
Think of being in heaven, and you must think of standing
in the very presence of God. He is the God of heaven.

Heaven is where God's glory is most wonderfully dis-
played

It would not be out of place to say that this is one of the
most significant and striking things which makes heaven

heaven. While well aware of a Scripture like Romans 1:20, speaking of the display of God's attributes in the world he has created, nevertheless it is in heaven supremely that every side, facet, aspect and lustre of God's glory – the glory of 'the God of glory' (Acts 7:2) – is most fully and most wonderfully displayed.

> My God, how wonderful Thou art,
> Thy majesty how bright!
> How beautiful Thy mercy-seat,
> In depths of burning light!
>
> F W Faber

You only have to let your eye pass through chapters 4 and 5 of Revelation to see that this is so.

Who is the God of heaven? What is he like?

His *majesty* (the royal one, 4:2). To speak of God's majesty is to express the thought of his greatness and to assert that to him alone is all worship, adoration and glory due.

> The Lord doth reign, and clothed is he
> With majesty most bright;
> His works do show him clothed to be,
> And girt about with might.
>
> Psalm 93:1 (metrical version)

The psalmist speaks of meditating on 'the glorious splendour of your majesty' (Ps. 145:5), and, in the same vein as the psalmist, the apostle Peter recalls how he and the other apostles 'were eye-witnesses of his majesty' (2 Pet. 1:16) as they gazed upon the Lord Jesus Christ, God's Messiah. Our place before God is to bow down before him in the dust, for he is in heaven and we are on earth, he is high and mighty and we are weak and lowly, he can do all things while without him we can do nothing, he dwells in brightness and spendour while we are invaded with sin.

His *sovereignty* (the reigning one, 4:2). The sovereignty of God – that God is sovereign – affirms his absolute, supreme and sole rule and authority over the whole of creation. He can do all things. He has no limitations. He is subject to no one. He does whatever pleases him. Of his own sovereignty, he declares, 'For I am God, and there is no other; I am God, and there is none like me, declaring the end from the beginning, and from ancient times things that are not yet done, saying, "My counsel shall stand, and I will do all my pleasure"' (Isa. 46:9f). All power belongs to him. He rules and reigns. It is customary to speak of God's sovereignty in terms of creation (God making the world), providence (God governing the world, the church and the lives of men) and grace (God saving sinners), all of which themes give great comfort to the believer who seeks to live the life of confidence and trust in God.

His *glory* (the precious stones, 4:3a). The word 'glory' in the Old Testament carried the sense of weight, worth and dignity. On one occasion Moses asked the Lord, 'Please, show me your glory' (Exod. 33:18). When shortly afterwards the Lord answered that request we read the words of 34:6-7, which give the sense of God's glory being a gathering together and revealing of all his divine attributes at once. He is glorious in himself. He is glorious in majesty, glorious in splendour, glorious in holiness, glorious in grace, glorious in justice, and so on. This glorious lustre attaches to and shines forth from everything about him. Supremely is the glory of God displayed 'in the face of Jesus Christ' (2 Cor. 4:6), who is 'the brightness of his glory and the express image of his person' (Heb. 1:3). The Lord Jesus Christ himself says, 'He who has seen me has seen the Father' (John 14:9).

His covenant mercy, grace and love (the rainbow, 4:3b). There is nothing in all the world to match this, and the rainbow encircling the throne is illustrative of it. Right back in Genesis 9, it was God's 'rainbow in the cloud' (9:13) which assured Noah and the little company of his family who had been kept safe in the ark from perishing in the universal flood, that God was determined to be gracious. 'But Noah found grace in the eyes of the LORD' (Gen. 6:8). He remains 'the God of all grace' (1 Pet. 5:10), who says to his people, 'Yes, I have loved you with an everlasting love; therefore with lovingkindness I have drawn you' (Jer. 31:3), and who 'to the praise of the glory of his grace ... has made us accepted in the Beloved' (Eph. 1:6). The essence of his grace is God acting graciously – despite our complete lack of any deserving and despite our awful record of sin against him. His is sovereign, eternal grace.

His *justice* (the awesome and terrible picture of 4:5). 'For the LORD is a God of justice' (Isa. 30:18). 'Righteousness and justice are the foundation of his throne' (Ps. 97:2). 'Shall not the Judge of all the earth do right?' (Gen. 18:25). This attribute points to the character of God as the Judge who, unlike any human judge, is always unswervingly and absolutely fair, just, wise, right and true. There are no flaws in his justice, and no questions or objections can ever be raised against it. He does all things well. He is proved right in everything he says and everything he does. Everything about his character guarantees his justice, and no finger can ever be pointed at him.

His *changelessness* (the sea of glass, 4:6). This detail of the vision speaks of the absence of any turmoil either in or with God. The changelessness (or immutability) of God has been spoken of as one of the excellencies of the Creator which distinguishes him from all his creatures. It is a magnificent theme. He is changeless in his whole being. He actually says, 'For I am the LORD, I do not change' (Mal. 3:6). He can change neither for the better nor for the worse, being continually absolutely perfect. With him 'there is no variation or shadow of turning' (Jas. 1:17). We never have cause to compare what he was like yesterday with what he is like today or what he will be like tomorrow. So he is entirely trustworthy, completely dependable and permanently faithful. Like himself, nothing of his truth, his ways, his purposes or his promises can ever change.

His *holiness* (the ascription of 4:8). What are we to say about God's holiness? We remarked earlier of his glory that all his divine attributes are gathered up in it at once. Of his holiness we may say that it permeates all his other attributes, such that his goodness is holy goodness, his love is holy love, his wrath is holy wrath, and so on. The root of God's holiness is his perfection, purity and beauty. 'There is none holy like the LORD, for there is none besides you', confessed Hannah in her prayer (1 Sam. 2:2). And we are commanded to 'worship the LORD in the beauty of holiness' (Ps. 29:2). He is 'of purer eyes than to behold evil, and cannot look on wickedness' (Hab. 1:13). And his demand of us is 'Be holy, for I am holy' (1 Pet. 1:16). Jonathan Edwards remarks, 'holiness is more than a mere attribute of God – it is the sum of all his attributes, the outshining of all that God is.'

His *eternity* (the assertion of 4:8). This is related to his changelessness but does not just say the same thing. Because God is eternal, he is changeless. 'Even from everlasting to everlasting you are God' (Ps. 90:2). He has no beginning and he has no end. He alone is the one 'who is and who was and who is to come, the Almighty' (Rev. 1:8). He never began to exist and he will never cease to exist. Eternity belongs only to him and is not something which any of his creatures have in common with him. 'The number of his years' cannot be discovered (Job 36:26). Indeed, his 'years will have no end' (Ps. 102:27). His very name, revealed to Moses, 'I AM WHO I AM' (Exod. 3:14), is intended to testify to his eternity.

His *'all-creatingness'* (the affirmation of 4:11). John Calvin has a famous statement about creation being the theatre of God's glory. This great statement here that God 'created all things' (which other Scriptures amplify so that we learn that God created all things out of nothing, in six days, by his divine word of command, for his own glory) is the centrepiece of this ascription of praise and worship to God with which chapter 4 ends. 'The heavens declare the glory of God; and the firmament shows his handiwork' (Ps. 19:1). 'For he spoke, and it was done; he commanded, and it stood fast' (Ps. 33:9). 'He gives to all life, breath, and all things' (Acts 17:25).

We learn all of that concerning the God of heaven from chapter 4! But what as we glance on into chapter 5? There the spotlight moves to God's own Son, the Lord Jesus Christ. For our present purposes, two more matters concerning the God of heaven shine forth here.

He is the *Redeeming one*. There is a threefold occurrence in chapter 5 of the verb 'slain': 'a Lamb as though it had been slain' (5:6), standing 'in the midst of the throne and of the four living creatures, and in the midst of the elders'; the statement concerning the Lamb, 'for you were slain, and have redeemed us to God by your blood out of every tribe and tongue and people and nation' (5:9); and 'the Lamb who was slain' who is 'worthy ... to receive power and riches and wisdom, and strength and honour and glory and blessing' (5:12).

The Lamb, of course, is a reference to the Lord Jesus Christ, and 'slain' refers to his sacrificial death upon the cross as an atonement and propitiation for sin. We are put in mind of John the Baptist's exclamation, 'Behold! The Lamb of God who takes away the sin of the world!' (John 1:29), and the apostle Paul's doctrinal statement, 'In him we have redemption through his blood, the forgiveness of sins, according to the riches of his grace' (Eph. 1:7). From the perspective of our present study, Revelation 5 is setting God forth as the redeeming God, the God who redeems us and reconciles us to himself. The basic meaning of 'redeem' or 'redemption' in Scripture is to buy back or deliver by payment of a price. Those who are the Lord's have been 'bought at a price' (1 Cor. 6:20), that price being the death and shed blood of God's own dear and spotless Son, our Saviour. Peter puts it this way: 'knowing that you were not redeemed with corruptible things, like silver or gold ... but with the precious blood of Christ, as of a lamb without blemish and without spot' (1 Pet. 1:18f). He 'himself bore our sins in his own body on the tree, that we, having died to sins, might live for righteousness' (1 Pet. 2:24).

> In His highest work, redemption,
> See His glory in a blaze;
> Nor can angels ever mention
> Aught that more of God displays.
> Grace and justice
> Here unite to endless days.   William Gadsby

He is *the Triune one*. In chapter 4 the emphasis falls upon God the Father. In chapter 5 the emphasis falls upon

God the Son. In addition to this, the reference in 4:5 to 'the seven spirits of God' is a reference to God the Holy Spirit in all the fulness and variety of his person and work. Among all the mysteries of Scripture, and all 'the depth of the riches both of the wisdom and knowledge of God' (Rom. 11:33), there is no mystery like that of the Trinity: that God is three, yet one – the three persons of the Godhead (Father, Son and Holy Spirit), yet only one God! We have to admit in this matter, with Isaac Watts, that 'where reason fails, with all her powers, there faith prevails, and love adores'. Scripture speaks very clearly of 'the name (singular: not 'names') of the Father and of the Son and of the Holy Spirit' (Matt. 28:19). The apostle Paul pronounces upon the Corinthians this benediction: 'The grace of the Lord Jesus Christ, and the love of God, and the communion of the Holy Spirit be with you all' (2 Cor. 13:14). The rich doctrine of the Trinity is most clearly expressed in the work of salvation (Eph. 1:3-14) and the privilege of prayer (Eph. 2:18).

Even after this brief and by no means exhaustive review of the display of God's glory in his nature and attributes (we have not begun to mention, for example, his faithfulness, goodness, love, patience, wrath, providence, wisdom, truth, or jealousy in any direct way, for it is not the intention of Revelation 4 and 5 to set out a systematic or complete doctrine of God), surely it is plain straightaway that our view and understanding of God is far, far too small. If you can put your knowledge of God into your pocket, if you can sum him up in a phrase, if you can box him up or file him away, if you ever think you have 'cracked' or mastered this doctrine, then you can be certain that your ideas of him are too small, too inadequate, too demeaning. The God of heaven is the one true and living God. He is the great God.

He is the glorious God. And there is no place where his greatness and glory is more fully or more wonderfully displayed than in heaven itself, as, by his grace, we shall see for ourselves when he takes his people there.

Heaven is filled with God's praise

We should hardly expect anything else after what we have discovered so far! It has often been expressed (and rightly) that theology, the very foundation and heart of which is the doctrine of God, should issue in doxology (praise, worship and adoration) as well as holiness of life. If that is so in our experience of God while we remain on earth, how much more will it be the case in heaven. Jonathan Edwards has a famous sermon at the end of his exposition of 1 Corinthians 13 called *Heaven a world of love*, and so it is. Equally, we may say that heaven is a world of praise – ceaseless praise, perfect praise, glorious praise, worthy praise, divine praise – because of who the God of heaven is.

Chapters 4 and 5 of Revelation bear testimony to this, as does the whole of the book. Heaven is filled with God's praise. We can formulate, in a summary manner, the following points:

Praise is due to God alone. There is a marked emphasis in 4:11 – 'You are worthy, O Lord' (NIV, 'You are worthy, our Lord and God') – the intention being to affirm 'You *alone* are worthy, *none but you* is worthy'. Worthy of what? Worthy 'to receive glory and honour and power', which, strictly, should be translated '*the* glory and *the* honour and *the* power' (why are the repeated definite articles missing from our English versions when they are so important?) God will not share his worship with another – not on earth, not in heaven, not now, not ever!

Praise is due to God from the whole of creation. 'For you created all things, and by your will they exist and were created', 4:11 continues. 'All your works shall praise you, O LORD' (Ps. 145:10). All God's works of creation, along with all the living creatures, including the heavenly hosts, render him praise. Follow through the verses: 4:8-9, 5:11,14.

Praise is due to God especially from his people. The verse just quoted from Psalm 145 continues, 'and your saints shall bless you'.

> Praise waits for thee in Zion, Lord:
> To thee vows paid shall be.
> O thou that hearer art of pray'r,
> All flesh shall come to thee.
>
> Ps. 65:1-2 (metrical version)

What is the special reason for this? God's people have been saved by his grace, having been chosen in Christ from all eternity, and have been 'redeemed ... to God by ... blood' (5:9). Follow through the verses: 4:10-11, 5:11-12,14.

Praise to God has at its very heart the adoration of his character. We traced out earlier some of the leading features of the God of heaven which are displayed in these two chapters, and he it is who is being worshipped and adored – not some unknown God, some hidden God, some unreal or concealed God, but the God who has made himself known in his Word, in his Son and in his world. Worship is 'worthship' – the declaration of God's worth. No other praise is worthy of him or acceptable to him.

Praise to God involves ascribing the same praise to the Son as is ascribed to the Father. This is made absolutely and unmistakably plain in 4:11 and then 5:12-13. The words of the Lord Jesus Christ himself further put it beyond doubt: '... all should honour the Son just as they honour the Father. He who does not honour the Son does not honour the Father who sent him' (John 5:23). How important this is in the face of so many (especially among the cults) who deny the deity of the Lord Jesus Christ.

What do you know of praising God? If you do not praise him on earth, how will you praise him in heaven? More starkly, if you are not among the company of those who, with a new, glad and spiritual heart, praise him on earth, what possible ground have you for assuming that you will ever praise him among the company of his people in heaven?

'Are the perfections of God the object of our delighted study? Do we love to gaze upon his holiness, till the soul melts and rejoices under its power? Since adoration is the nature of this spiritual life, so that it can no more cease to adore than a living man to breathe, we may by this judge of its vigour in our own hearts. We may thus discover also a secret cause of our own spiritual weakness. For as this is the essential nature of true religion, the habitual direction of the soul to this great object in meditation, and prayer, and praise is absolutely necessary to preserve a vigorous Christian life'.[2]

Stephen Charnock on the God of heaven

Stephen Charnock (1628-1680) was a Puritan minister, and one-time assistant to John Owen. He was one of those ministers ejected from their charges at the time of the restoration of Charles II, when the Act was published which required a perfect conformity to the Book of Common Prayer, and to all the rites and ceremonies of the established church. One writer has opined that the effect of that enactment (on 24 August 1662, 'Black Bartholomew's Day') was 'the silencing of nearly 2,500 ministers, the death of 3,000 non-conformists, and the ruin of 60,000 families'.[3]

Apart from his own part in these sufferings, it has been said of Charnock that his life, 'in contrast to the turbulence of England in the mid-seventeenth century, was almost uneventful'.[4] The brief facts seem to be these: he was educated at Cambridge University; he ministered in Southwark, was a Fellow and then a Senior Proctor at Oxford University; in 1655 he went to Dublin as chaplain to the Governor of Ireland (Henry Cromwell, one of Oliver Cromwell's sons); and then (in 1675, restrictions on reformed ministers having relaxed somewhat) he ministered at a church in Crosby Square, London, alongside another esteemed Puritan minister, Thomas Watson. Of this pairing, Spurgeon has remarked: 'What two shepherds for the flock! Men of such most extraordinary gifts and graces were seldom if ever united in one pastorate.'

A most significant statement of Charnock's is this: 'It is impossible to honour God as we ought, unless we know him as he is.' Out of all his writings, he is best remembered for his major work entitled *Discourses on the Existence and Attributes of God*, written in 1681-2. It is from this that the following three extracts are taken.

Hear him first upon *the holiness of God*. 'As it seems to challenge an excellency above all his other perfections, so it is the glory of all the rest; as it is the glory of the God-head, so it is the glory of every perfection in the Godhead; as his power is the strength of them, so his holiness is the beauty of them; as all would be weak without almightiness to back them, so all would be uncomely without holiness to adorn them. Should this be sullied, all the rest would lose their honour and their comfortable efficacy; as at the same instant that the sun should lose its light, it would lose its heat, its strength, its generative and quickening virtue. As sincerity is the lustre of every grace in a Christian, so is purity the splendour of every attribute in the Godhead. His justice is a holy justice, his wisdom a holy wisdom, his arm of power a "holy arm" (Ps. 98:1), his truth or promise a "holy promise" (Ps. 105:42). Holy and true go hand in hand (Rev. 6:10). "His name", which signifies all his attributes in conjunction, "is holy" (Ps. 103:1)). Yea, he is "righteous in all his ways, and holy in all his works" (Ps. 145:17). It is the rule of all his acts, the source of all his punishments. If every attribute of the Deity were a distinct member, purity would be the form, the soul, the spirit to animate them. Without it, his patience would be an indulgence to sin, his mercy a fondness, his wrath a madness, his power a tyranny, his wisdom an unworthy subtilty. It is this gives decorum to all.'

Now hear him on *the patience of God*. Dealing with the question as to why God exercises so much patience, Charnock lists various reasons before coming to this – for the continuance of the church. 'If he be not patient towards sinners, what stock would there be for believers to spring up from? He bears with the provoking carriage of men, evil men; because out of their loins he intends to extract others, which he will form for the glory of his grace. He hath some unborn, that belong to the "election of grace", which are to be the seed of the worst of men. Jeroboam, the chief incendiary of the Israelites to idolatry, had an Abijah, in whom was found "some good thing towards the Lord God of Israel" (1 Kgs. 14:13). Had Ahaz been snapped in the first act of his wickedness, the Israelites had wanted so good a prince, and so good a man as Hezekiah, a branch of that wicked predecessor. What gardener cuts off the thorns from the rose-bush till he hath gathered the roses? And men do not use to burn all the crab tree, but preserve a stock to engraft some sweet fruit upon. There could not have been a saint on earth, nor consequently in heaven, had it not been for this perfection.'

Hear him, finally, on *the goodness of God*, in a passage where he is dealing with God's own pleasure in communicating his goodness. 'Moses desired to see his glory, God assures him he should see his goodness (Exod. 33:18-19), intimating that his goodness is his glory, and his glory his delight also. He sends not forth his blessings with an ill will; he doth not stay till they are squeezed from him ... he is most delighted when he is most diffusive, and his pleasure in bestowing is larger than his creatures' in possessing; he is not covetous of his own treasures; he lays up his goodness in order to laying it out with a complacency wholly divine ... God's foresight of the ill use men would make of his benefits damped him not in bestowing his largesses ... None can overtop him in goodness, because nothing hath any good, but what is derived from him; his gifts are without repentance ... What God gives out of goodness he gives with joy and gladness ... He beheld the world after its creation with a complacency, and still governs it with the same pleasure wherewith he reviewed it. Infinite cheerfulness attends infinite goodness.'

2

THE PURITY OF HEAVEN

This is a book about heaven. So let me address a very direct question to you who are reading it, before we proceed any further. Are you going to heaven? Will we meet one another there?

I ask for a reason. There is often an assumption made that everyone will get to heaven, one way or another, in the end. The world is full of people who (insofar as they think about it at all) imagine that they are going to heaven. They have no fears to the contrary, and are quite confident in the matter. Year in and year out funerals take place at which ministers (who should know better) pronounce firmly and confidently about this one and that one having arrived safely in heaven when, frankly, such firmness and confidence (in many cases) is without any clear ground. The subject comes up from time to time on television and radio discussion programmes when, once again, this presumption is entertained, and the whole cast of all that is said is along the lines of 'when I get to heaven', as if there can be no doubt about everyone being there.

Yet the assumption is a false one and (because the matter itself is of such important and eternal dimensions) a tragic one. It is false because of the vital distinction stated in the verse from the book of Revelation which we shall focus upon in this chapter. The verse is 21:27 and reads as follows: 'But there shall by no means enter it anything that defiles, or causes an abomination or a lie, but only those who are written in the Lamb's book of life.'

'By no means' is a very strong expression. The AV translates it 'in no wise', while the NIV fails to bring out its
force adequately at all. Then later in the verse is the phrase
'but only those' (AV has 'but', NIV has 'but only'); you
could translate it 'except, but for, apart from'. The point to
make is that this is very discriminating language. It speaks
of those who are in and those who are out, those who are
admitted and those who are not, those who have a place
and those who do not. You cannot sidestep the issue. The
phrases chosen by the Holy Spirit at this point in the Scriptures cannot be avoided. They will not go away. They look
us in the eye. They face us with the truth. God himself has
put them there. The crucial fact is this: some people will be
in heaven, and some people will not be in heaven. Those
who are in will be in. Those who are out will be out. And
the reason for it all? The purity of heaven.

Revelation 21 records another of the magnificent visions
given to the apostle John during the course of his exile on
the island of Patmos 'for the word of God and for the testimony of Jesus Christ' (1:9) – that is to say, for his unflinch-
ing faithfulness to that divine word and testimony. Observe
how this chapter 21 begins. John sees something. 'And I
saw a new heaven and a new earth, for the first heaven and
the first earth had passed away. Also there was no more
sea.' That is the first thing, but there is more immediately.
'Then I, John, saw the holy city, new Jerusalem, coming
down out of heaven from God, prepared as a bride adorned
for her husband.'

Now this 'holy city, new Jerusalem' is the glorified
church of the Lord Jesus Christ. It is 'that perfected company of the elect and sanctified', says Spurgeon. It is (in

Cowper's lines) 'all the ransomed church of God ... saved to sin no more'. However, at the same time and in consequence of this, the teaching of this 21st chapter is teaching about heaven. As its verses unfold and we learn about the glory of the church, so we are directed to the glory of heaven. As we contemplate the security of the church with its walls, its gates and its foundations, we find ourselves contemplating the security of heaven. As we delight at the prospect of the fellowship of the church with God, so our souls begin to thrill at the thought of the very nature and substance of the life of heaven being God dwelling among his people. And as we learn about the purity of the glorified church (her holiness through and through), so we are confronted with the thing so easily forgotten (or, maybe, never even thought of at all by many): the purity of heaven, what a holy place heaven is, and how only those who are holy can ever enter it, while all who are not holy are excluded from it.

Nothing of this, mind you, should surprise us after all we learned in the opening chapter. Just take a moment to recall those three principles concerning heaven which we laid down from chapters 4 and 5: heaven is God's dwelling place; it is the place where his glory is most fully displayed; and the whole of heaven is filled with God's praise. So how could such a place ever be anything other than holy and pure? If such a thing should surprise you as you read it, that is a reminder that a fundamental reason behind people's false ideas of heaven and their false assumptions that they are automatically heading there, is that they think of 'the next life' (as they think of 'the present life') in man-centred terms (their own and others' ideas and opinions) rather than in the light of the clear teaching of the word of God.

The barrier in place

Barriers bar the way. It might merely be a barrier across the entrance to a car park; but if the barrier is in place you cannot drive in, whether you wish to or not. What the first part of 21:27 speaks of is a great barrier which shuts men, women, boys and girls out of heaven. It is the barrier of man's sin.

This is not the only occasion when the Bible speaks of sin in this way. Go right back to the beginning and recall the record of the fall of Adam and Eve into sin, following their disobedience to God. Genesis 3:23f speaks of a barrier: 'therefore the LORD God sent him (Adam) out of the garden of Eden ... So he drove out the man; and he placed cherubim at the east of the garden of Eden, and a flaming sword which turned every way, to guard the way to the tree of life.'

The prophet Isaiah speaks of a barrier. 'But your iniquities have separated you from your God; and your sins have hidden his face from you, so that he will not hear' (59:2). Moreover, in a section of the New Testament where the Lord Jesus Christ is teaching very clearly about the last judgment, this is what he says: 'And while they went to buy, the bridegroom came, and those who were ready went in with him to the wedding; and the door was shut' (Matt. 25:10). There, in the parable of the wise and foolish virgins, he is speaking of a barrier.

So it is in line with such Scriptures as these (by way of example) that the verse we are focusing on in the book of Revelation (21:27) is to be understood. It declares the presence of a barrier, the purpose and effect of which is to keep out of the glorified church in heaven 'anything that defiles, or causes an abomination or a lie'. The several different parts of that phrase need to be examined in turn.

First, there is the mention of '*anything that defiles*' (NIV has 'impure'). Heaven would be ruined by defilement. It is unthinkable to conceive of heaven's glory ever being dimmed by the taint of our sin. Think again of that description of God in the prophecy of Habakkuk, that he is 'of purer eyes than to behold evil, and cannot look on wickedness' (1:13). Then there is the strong statement of the apostle John in his first letter: 'God is light and in him is no darkness at all' (1:5). In the same vein, the apostle Paul presses the great questions which are not without application to the case in point, 'For what fellowship has righteousness with lawlessness? And what communion has light with darkness? And what accord has Christ with Belial? Or what part has a believer with an unbeliever? And what agreement has the temple of God with idols?' (2 Cor. 6:14-16).

In all of this we are face to face with the fact (I say, the fact) that there is no place in heaven for defiled lives, impure hearts, unclean minds, unholy bodies or crooked tongues. It even extends to this: not even any wish, desire, hunger, leaning, inclination, thought, or imagination of evil will be found in heaven, still less any sinful deed actually performed. Nothing will ever be done inside those gates of pearl which is contrary to God's perfect law or in opposition to God's spotless holiness. The world and its worldliness have no place in heaven. The flesh and its lustfulness have no place in heaven. The proud and their arrogance have no place in heaven. The self-righteous and their contentedness with themselves have no place in heaven. The sinner and his sinfulness have no place in heaven, however outwardly decent, respected in society, or famed in history. 'But there shall by no means enter it anything that defiles.'

Second, we read of *'anything that ... causes an abomination'* (NIV has 'anyone who does what is shameful'). You would think, from what men say and write and the applause which greets them, that there is no such thing as an abomination any more. Certainly we live in days when, in many quarters, nothing is considered shameful – days which, sadly, merit again that description of life as it was in the Old Testament days recorded in the book of Judges when 'everyone did what was right in his own eyes' (17:6). Men call good evil and evil good. They are 'not at all ashamed', nor do 'they know how to blush' (Jer. 6:15). Much of the blame for all of this lies with the proponents of evolutionary theory, which has got such a grip on the hearts and minds of so many, and which (so conveniently for them) puts God out of the picture. Yet, notwithstanding it all, men still reckon on going to heaven!

Of this phrase in our verse, J C Ryle comments: 'This touches the case of all who practise those sins of life which God has pronounced abominable, and take pleasure in them, and countenance those who practise them. These are the men who work the works of the flesh, each as his heart inclines him. These are the adulterers, fornicators, and unclean livers; these are the drunkards, revellers, and gluttons; these are the blasphemers, swearers, and liars. These are the men who count it no shame to live in hatred, variance, wrath, strife, envyings, quarrellings and the like. They throw the reins on the neck of their lusts; they follow their passions wherever they may lead them; their only object is to please themselves.'[5]

A number of New Testament passages bear upon this matter of those who cause an abomination. In the book of

Revelation itself, 21:8 and 22:15 are particularly significant, gathering up as they do such abominations before God as unbelief, murder, sexual immorality, sorcery, and idolatry. Several other Scriptures are also worthy of special note. Romans 1:18ff commences with the principle that 'the wrath of God is revealed from heaven against all ungodliness and unrighteousness of men, who suppress the truth in unrighteousness', and then proceeds to work that out in some detail (of great contemporary relevance, for example, to sexual perversion). Then there is the insistence in 1 Corinthians 6:9-10 that 'neither fornicators, nor idolaters, nor adulterers, nor homosexuals, nor sodomites, nor thieves, nor covetous, nor drunkards, nor revilers, nor extortioners will inherit the kingdom of God' (though do not fail to look on to the next verse, 6:11, with its wonderful display of saving and transforming grace: 'And such were some of you. But you were washed, but you were sanctified, but you were justified in the name of the Lord Jesus and by the Spirit of our God'). Further, a portion like 2 Timothy 3:1-4, with its reminder 'that in the last days perilous times will come', and its exposition of some of the leading characteristics of such times, is also of great significance.

Concerning all the people who bear the character of our verse, folk may exalt their names, read their books, watch their films and television programmes, buy their records, follow their fashions, imitate their lifestyle, and so on. Yet the fact remains: no one who 'causes an abomination' will have any part or place in heaven. By no means!

Third, we read of '*anything that ... causes ... a lie*' (NIV has 'deceitful'). Anything false, untrue, deceptive, hypocritical, erroneous, mistaken, suspicious, unreal or any such thing can never enter this holy heaven. There can be no falsehood, no untruth, for only truth can dwell with the God of truth. There can be no lying and no cover-up; none 'having a form of godliness but denying its power' (2 Tim. 3:5); none who profess what they do not practise, speak what they do not believe, talk to you of grace but show nothing of the reality of it in their lives; none who announce that they believe in God but show no desire to learn of him, glorify him, enjoy him, walk with him or be made like him.

Does this appear to you to be a fierce text? Yet it is for our good that it should be so, for we cannot afford to be deceived upon such a matter as this. The things we have considered so far should drive us to examine our lives, our hearts and our ways – and to desire the Lord himself, the God of heaven, to examine us before it is too late and we face his final examination with no space or opportunity left for repentance. The barrier is firmly in place. Well might we reflect: can such a barrier ever be dealt with? We are reminded of the question the disciples once asked the Lord Jesus Christ: 'Who then can be saved?' (Mark 10:26).

The barrier removed

Thankfully, there is a second part to 21:27, and to it we now come with some relief. Who may enter into the purity of heaven? We are told, 'but only those who are written in the Lamb's book of life'. On the surface this looks very puzzling. There is a mention of names written in a book. The book is named; it is 'the Lamb's book of life'. What book is that? The answer is that it is a secret book belonging to God himself, in which have been written from before the foundation of the world the names of all those whom it would be God's sovereign pleasure to save from their sins, reconcile to himself, remove every barrier to their entrance into heaven and bring them safely there. He has chosen them.

Several grand Scriptures come to mind. There is Ephesians 1:4, which sets forth this matter of God's choice (or
election) in these words: 'just as he chose us in him' (that
is, just as the Father chose us in the Son) 'before the foundation of the world, that we should be holy and without
blame before him in love.' There is 2 Timothy 2:19, which
asserts that 'the solid foundation of God stands, having this
seal: "The Lord knows those who are his".' And there is
Romans 8:30, with its magnificent statement: 'Moreover
whom he predestined, these he also called; whom he called,
these he also justified; and whom he justified, these he also
glorified.' In other words, here is a people of God's choice,
a people for God's possession, the work of his hand, for the
display of his splendour. However, the book in which their
names are written ('the Lamb's book of life') is secret.

You might wish to put the question: what is the point of
mentioning this book, then, if we cannot read the names of
those who are written in it? If the whole thing is classified,
top secret material; if it is so shrouded in mystery; if we
cannot get access to it to view it and go through it – what
help is it even to know of its existence? Is this a riddle? Are
we being teased? Certainly not!

It is exceedingly helpful to learn of this book. Let me tell
you why. Although we cannot handle the book for ourselves
and read the names, we may know clearly from the Bible
the character of those whose names are written there and
who will enter heaven – which is the very thing we need to
know in order to discover how we stand in the matter. What
is that character? Let me set it out by way of the following
assertions.

Those whose names are written in 'the Lamb's book of

life' are these. They know God is holy and that they are
sinners who cannot stand in his pure sight. They have acknowledged that their sins have quite rightly barred them
from God's presence, and know they have no worthiness or
merit of their own before him, and deserve only to be condemned by him. They know what it is to hate their sin, to
mourn over it, to turn from it with godly sorrow in repentance and shame, and to forsake their sin. They have cried
out to God for mercy and forgiveness, knowing that without it and but for it they have no hope and are absolutely
finished. They are believers in God's Son ('the Lamb'), for
they have trusted him in the work that he has done, once for
all, to save them – dying on the cross at Calvary to bear
their sins, their guilt and their punishment in their place.
They have no boast or confidence anymore apart from
Christ, and God the Father has accepted them in his beloved Son. They have been what the Bible calls 'born again',
and have become a new creation in the Lord Jesus Christ,
with old things having passed away and all things having
become new. As a result, although they still struggle with
their sins, get into various scrapes and face many trials,
they now have a heart for God, a desire to please him by
obeying all that he asks of them in his word, a passion for
holiness (to be holy as he is holy), and a deep heart longing
to be with him in heaven, his holy dwelling. None of those
whatsoever is due to any works of theirs. That could never
be. It is all, entirely, of God's pure and free grace. They
have discovered that 'the wages of sin is death, but the gift
of God is eternal life in Christ Jesus our Lord' (Rom. 6:23).
They live every moment of their lives in continual and utter
amazement at the goodness of God towards them.

I could tell you much more about them, because the Bible

has so much more to say, but that will have to do. Do you get the picture? The question for you is this: are you among them? Are you sure you are among them? Are you positive you are among them?

Consider once more this verse, 21:27. What a crowd the first part of the verse keeps out! What a company the second part of the verse welcomes in! Behold here the purity of heaven. It really is a case of 'no holiness – no heaven'. It cannot be any other way. Here is Spurgeon again. 'Imagine for a moment that the decree of our text were reversed or suspended, and that it were allowed that a few unregenerate men and women (ie, those not born again) should enter into the glorified church of God ... How could heaven bear with these? ... It must not be ... All heaven is up in arms at the supposition ... Heaven were not heaven if it were possible for evil of any sort to enter there.' And here is Ryle once again as well. 'God will not alter heaven merely to please you; better a thousand times to conform to his ways while you can. You must love the things of heaven before your death, or else you cannot enter heaven when you die.'

> There is a city bright;
> Closed are its gates to sin;
>   Nought that defileth,
>   Nought that defileth
> Can ever enter in.
>
> Saviour, I come to Thee!
> O Lamb of God, I pray,
>   Cleanse me and save me,
>   Cleanse me and save me,
> Wash all my sins away.
>
> Lord, make me from this hour,
> Thy loving child to be;

Kept by Thy power,
Kept by Thy power
From all that grieveth thee.

Till in the snowy dress
Of Thy redeemed I stand,
Faultless and stainless,
Faultless and stainless,
Safe in that happy land!

Mary Ann Sanderson Deck

Thomas Brooks on the purity of heaven
Thomas Brooks (1608-1680) was one of the most popular
preachers in London during the days of Cromwell and the
interregnum. A fellow-minister and friend said of him, 'he
had a body of divinity in his head and the power of it in his
heart'. Another friend, and companion in sufferings, John
Reeve, when preaching his funeral sermon, spoke of him
as 'a person of a very sweet nature and temper ... a very
great gravity ... a very large charity ... a wonderful patience
... a very strong faith in the promises of both worlds'. He
added this: 'And now he is at rest. And though he is gone,
he is not lost; he is yet useful to the church of God, and
being dead he yet speaks by his example and writings, which
were very profitable and spiritual.'

He attended Emmanuel College, Cambridge (that blessed
gathering place of Puritan company in those days!) in 1625.
Between Cambridge and being licensed as a preacher of
the gospel, he seems to have spent some years at sea, probably as a chaplain with the fleet. He ministered in London,
first at Thomas Apostles (during which time he was chosen
to preach before the House of Commons on 26 December
1648), and then at St Margaret's, Fish-Street Hill (where he
encountered opposition over his refusal of those whom he

considered unfit for baptism and the Lord's Supper). He married twice, the second time being in 1677-8, 'she spring-young, he winter-old'.

His collected works fill six choice volumes, and include *Precious Remedies against Satan's Devices, Heaven on Earth, Apples of Gold, The Mute Christian under the Smarting Rod, The Unsearchable Riches of Christ, The Privy Key of Heaven, An Ark for all God's Noahs*, and much else besides, many (as the aforementioned illustrate) with striking and attractive titles.

The entire fourth volume of his works is entitled *The Crown and Glory of Christianity: or Holiness, The only way to Happiness*, taking as its text Hebrews 12:14 ('Follow peace with all men, and holiness, without which no man shall see the Lord', AV). He subtitles the work, *The Necessity, Excellency, Rarity, and Beauty of Holiness*. From this, the following extracts are taken.

'God hath by very plain and clear scriptures bolted and barred the door of heaven and happiness against all unholy ones. Witness 1 Corinthians 6:9-10.... Heaven is an undefiled inheritance, and none that are defiled can enter into the possession of it, 1 Peter 1:4. When the angels fell from their righteousness, heaven rejected them; it would no longer hold them; and will it now accept of the unrighteous? Will it now entertain and welcome them? Surely no. Such sinners make the very earth to mourn and groan now; and shall they make heaven to mourn and groan hereafter? Surely no. What though the serpent did wind himself into an earthly paradise, yet none of the seed of the serpent, so remaining, shall ever be able to wind themselves into a heavenly paradise. Witness Galatians 5:19-21 ...'

In dealing in a thorough manner with reasons why 'without

real holiness there is no happiness', Brooks comes to this: 'Because unholy persons have no hearts to go to heaven. Though now and then they may talk of heaven, and now and then lift up their eyes and hands to heaven, and now and then express a few cold wishes and lazy desires after heaven, it is no difficult thing to demonstrate that in good earnest they have no heart to go to heaven.' That demonstration he proceeds to give by way of ten questions, one after the other, as follows.

'How often hath God set life and death, heaven and hell before them, and they have chosen death rather than life, and hell rather than heaven? Do you think that that man hath any heart to heaven, that will not so much as part with a lust for heaven? ... that hath not so much as a hand to lay hold on the opportunities of grace that might bring him to heaven? ... that daily hardens his heart against him who is the way to heaven? ... who is still a-grieving, vexing, and quenching that Spirit of holiness, that only can fit, frame and form him for heaven? ... that rarely spends a serious thought of heaven, and that lives in this world as if there were no heaven? ... whose sinful courses speak him out to be one of those who have made a covenant with death, and an agreement with hell? ... that detests those most that are the best wooers for heaven? ... who can take no pleasure or delight in those that are travelling towards heaven? ... that will do nothing affectionately for heaven; that will not hear for heaven, nor pray for heaven, nor trade for heaven, nor look for heaven, nor long for heaven, nor strive for heaven, nor wait for heaven?'

Hear him again. 'Heaven would be a very hell to an unholy heart. If now the presence of God in his servants, and the presence of God in his ordinances, be such a hell to unholy souls, ah, what a hell would the presence of God in heaven be to unholy hearts! It is true an unholy heart may desire heaven, as it is a place of freedom from troubles, afflictions, oppressions, vexations, etc., but this is the least and lowest part of heaven; but to desire it as it is, a place of purity, of grace, of holiness, of enjoying of God, etc., is above the reach of an unholy heart. The company of heaven are all holy, the employments of heaven are all holy, and the enjoyments of heaven are all holy; and therefore heaven cannot but be an undesirable thing to unholy hearts. An unholy heart is no ways desirous nor ambitious of such a heaven as will rid him of his darling sins, as will make him conformable to a holy God, as will everlastingly divorce him from his old companions, and link him for ever to those gracious souls that he hath scorned, despised, and persecuted in this world.'

In treating the question how we may 'know whether we have this real holiness or no', 'whether God hath sown this heavenly seed in our souls or no', Brooks answers, 'there are several ways whereby this may be discovered'. The points he follows with include these: 'A person of real holiness is much affected and taken up in the admiration of the holiness of God ... True holiness is diffusive ... it spreads itself over head and heart, lip and life, inside and outside ... Persons of real holiness do set the highest price and the greatest value and esteem upon those that are holy ... He that is truly holy will be still a-reaching and stretching himself out after higher degrees of holiness; yea, a man that is truly holy, can never be holy enough ... Where there is real holiness, there is a holy hatred, detestation, and indignation against all ungodliness and wickedness ... He that is truly holy will labour and endeavour to make others holy ... True holiness is conformable to the holiness of Christ.'

3

THE WAY TO HEAVEN

How can you ever expect to get anywhere if you don't know the right way? Just think, for example, of travelling from York to London or from York to Edinburgh. 'Ah!', you say, 'that's straightforward enough; after all, all roads south from York must lead to London, and all roads north from York must lead to Edinburgh. I'm bound to get there easily enough – no need to give it much advance thought. I'll just strike out in the correct general direction and then I'm bound to pick up a sign sooner or later. I can check the map sometime if I need to. Or I can always stop and ask someone. There won't be any problem'.

But is it not much better and wiser, and likely to save you a considerable amount of trouble, to discover the way you should travel before you set out, lest even in your earliest turnings you make a mistake? Surely it is important right at the beginning to know not only *where* you desire to go, but *how* you are going to get there. It is the case, of course, where London and Edinburgh are concerned, that there are a variety of routes which you could take from York, some direct and some less direct, some functional and some more scenic, and so on. In that case, it will not matter quite so much which one you choose, so long as there is no question about you not getting there in the end. If you were really determined, you could even travel from York to London via Edinburgh. It would certainly be the long way round, and a most peculiar way of making the journey. But it would be possible, if you had plenty of time, and wanted to see as many places as possible on the way!

However, we are concerned in this chapter with a journey which is very different from and far more important than any journey you might ever make anywhere on the face of the globe. It is the journey to heaven. Life itself is a journey. You are alive, and so you are journeying. There are only two possible destinations at the end of life's journey. One is heaven. One is hell. We are concerned here with the way to heaven. Do you desire to go to heaven? If you do, have you considered how you are going to get there? The great point not to be missed is this: *there is only one way to heaven*. Let me emphasise that: there is only one way to heaven. It is not like the journeys mentioned in the earlier paragraphs, where you can engage in a certain amount of picking and choosing which route you prefer or which way suits you best. Where York, London and Edinburgh are concerned there is flexibility and variety. That is not the case, however, with the journey from earth to heaven. There is only one way.

The key text in the book of Revelation which sets this out for us is 7:13-14. 'Then one of the elders answered, saying to me, "Who are these arrayed in white robes, and where did they come from?" And I said to him, "Sir, you know." So he said to me, "These are the ones who come out of the great tribulation, and washed their robes and made them white in the blood of the Lamb."' Maybe we can best approach this vital subject by means of putting to the verses four straightforward questions. The apostle John, here, is experiencing another of the remarkable visions with which the whole of Revelation abounds. He is being given amazing views of spiritual, heavenly and eternal things.

Who did John see?

Quite clearly he saw a company of people wearing white robes. We are informed that 'one of the elders' put a question to John concerning what he saw, asking him the identity of 'these arrayed in white robes'. These white robes speak of the character and standing before God of those who are wearing them. White is the colour of immaculate purity, indicating the complete absence of any fault or flaw. It is the colour which signifies triumph and victory. It speaks of unspeakable joy. It is the colour of bridal array. So who are these who John sees dressed in this fashion? They comprise the very same company who have already been described earlier in the chapter in verses 9 and 10 – 'a great multitude which no one could number, of all nations, tribes, peoples, and tongues, standing before the throne and before the Lamb, clothed with white robes, with palm branches in their hands, and crying out with a loud voice, saying, "Salvation belongs to our God who sits on the throne, and to the Lamb!"' Notice that very striking and vigorous sequence of verbs: standing, wearing, holding, crying out.

Who are they? There is only one answer. Here is the church of God. John is looking, symbolically, at the people of God, all gathered together. None of them is missing, none forgotten, none left out, none absent. There they all are.

Where had they come from?

The elder puts this very question to John: 'where did they come from?'. Moreover, it is this same elder who then supplies the answer to the apostle. 'These are the ones who come out of the great tribulation.' What does that mean?

It means that they have come out of the world that is full of sin and trial and danger. They have been kept safe while they were journeying through it, and have now been delivered safely from it. They have left it all behind. It is now in the past. They have left this earthly scene of time altogether. They have vacated their places here. They no longer dwell in this vale of tears. Even while they did, they were constantly on the move, continually passing through. They never really belonged here at all. This was not their home, their abiding place. They were never here to stay. They were pilgrims. This was not their enduring city. They were heading elsewhere. They had a destination in view. While here on earth they faced many difficulties, for they experienced repeatedly the truth that 'we must through many tribulations enter the kingdom of God' (Acts 14:22). They knew many dark days. Many a time, no doubt, they were at their wits' end, their strength failing, their hearts sinking, their enemies abounding. But not any more! 'These are the ones who come out of the great tribulation', that indicating not some one specific trial but being a larger and comprehensive reference to the whole scene or realm of tribulation and trouble. Indeed, the reference to the tribulation is strictly 'the tribulation, the great one', further underscoring its all-inclusiveness. It is the one long tribulation endured by all of God's servants in every age. All of their persecutions, trials and afflictions are included in it.

No longer are they here upon the earth. The verb translated 'come out' is literally 'the ones coming out' or 'the coming out ones' – what is known as a 'timeless present', in order to indicate the total number of those who come from every generation.

Where are they?

I mean: where are they as John views them, now that they have left tribulation behind? The answer, in a word, is: in heaven. This is confirmed by reference back to 4:1-2, where we are told that John 'looked, and behold, a door standing open in heaven', through which he then proceeded to view all that was revealed to him; and also in connection with 7:9, already observed, where these same folk who appear in our present verse are pictured as 'standing before the throne', and heaven is the only possible location for the divine throne.

John is looking into heaven, then, and so doing sees not only the throne of God, with the angels standing around it and the elders and the four living creatures falling on their faces before the throne and worshipping God, but also this vast company standing before it as well, and the whole inhabitants together joining in the praises of God: 'Salvation belongs to our God who sits on the throne, and to the Lamb!'

So then: what have we discovered so far?

Who did John see? The people of God, the church, the redeemed ones, the saved multitude.

Where had they come from? The earth, with all its trials.

Where are they? In heaven, before the throne of God.

All of which brings us to the crunch question:

How did they get there?

We are concerned to know the way to heaven. Since, as we observed to begin with, the Bible makes it plain that there is only one way to heaven, the answer to our present question (how did the folk here in 7:13-14 get to heaven?) will give us the answer to the pressing and personal question, 'how may you and I get there?'

The answer we are looking for is found in verse 14. 'These are the ones who come out of the great tribulation, and washed their robes and made them white in the blood of the Lamb.' This takes us to the very heart of the matter. Let us take it step-by-step, in three stages.

(1) *Defilement*. The statement they have 'washed their robes' clearly implies that previously they were defiled, unclean, stained, dirty and filthy. So they were. So we all are. So is all mankind. This is how we are by nature. It is our natural state, just as we are. Indeed, it describes us even as we were conceived in our mother's womb, let alone since we have actually been born.

This problem is the problem of our sin. 'For there is no difference; for all have sinned and fall short of the glory of God' (Rom. 3:22f). The point is made even earlier in the same chapter, where the apostle Paul quotes from the Old Testament. 'There is no one righteous, no, not one' (3:10).

Somehow in our day we seem to have lost any true sense and understanding of what sin really is, and the condition and extremity that we are all in as sinners. It is worth taking a moment to explain things. There is a verse in the New Testament (1 John 3:4) which gives a clear definition of sin in one word: 'sin is lawlessness'. You could translate it with the phrase 'transgression of the law'. If you trangress, you cross the line, you break the rules, you go beyond the bounds, you miss the target, you abandon the path, you defy the authority.

This is the killer disease that has got a hold upon us all. The slightest transgression of God's law and commandments, the minutest departure from God's spotless holiness, the tiniest shortfall from God's unbending standards is sin. Do you know anything of yourself and your own heart and life? Can you not see the truth of Paul's classic statement from Romans 3 just quoted above? Sin has affected all mankind. Yet that is not all. It has affected every part of us (our minds, our hearts, our bodies, our consciences, our wills, our affections, everything). Hence the appropriateness of the diagnosis given in Isaiah's prophecy: 'The whole head is sick, and the whole heart faints. From the sole of the foot even to the head, there is no soundness in it, but wounds and bruises and putrefying sores; they have not been closed or bound up, or soothed with ointment' (1:5f).

Does sin have any effect? Most certainly it does! It defiles us before the holy God. It pronounces us guilty before the holy God. It separates us from the holy God. It condemns us before the holy God. It leaves us, in and of ourselves, helpless before the holy God. You will notice the deliberate and repeated emphasis there: sin ruins us before God, for God is holy.

Such *was* the condition of those whom John saw, *before* they had washed their robes.

(2) *Cleansing*. Stay with the phrase 'washed their robes' a little longer. Surely it implies that these once defiled ones have now been cleansed from their defilement. If that is so, then (in the light of what we have just learned of sin and its effects) the related problems of their guilt, separation, condemnation and helplessness must have been dealt with as well. For here they are in heaven, with God, standing before his throne, accepted before him and praising his name.

How can this be? How is it possible? The statement that they have 'washed their robes and made them white in the blood of the Lamb' tells us all we need to know. At the centre there is that word 'blood'. Blood usually causes a stain. Indeed there is nothing quite like blood for doing that. You only have to think of a cut finger wrapped in a handkerchief or a nose bleed. The point, though, is this. You do not expect to wash in blood something that is already defiled, and then, having done so, find that it comes out white and pure, fresh and clean. That is the very thing that has happened here, though. These ones in heaven: their defiled robes have been washed in blood and now, in consequence, are white! That is what the Scripture declares! There is no way round it.

What, then, is this remarkable blood? We would do better to ask, '*whose* blood is it?' We are told precisely. It is 'the blood of the Lamb', and we already know who the Lamb is. He is the Lord Jesus Christ, God's own Son, the Saviour of sinners. His very name testifies to this, for on the occasion when the angel of the Lord appeared in a dream to Joseph, prior to the coming of the Son of God to earth, this is what he said of what was about to happen, and with particular reference to his name: 'And she (Mary) will bring forth a son, and you shall call his name Jesus, for he will save his people from their sins' (Matt. 1:21).

His coming to save is declared in the Bible again and again. One celebrated verse is this: 'This is a faithful saying and worthy of all acceptance, that Christ Jesus came into the world to save sinners, of whom I am chief', writes the apostle Paul (1 Tim. 1:15). How has he done that? How has he saved sinners? He has done it by dying upon the cross at Calvary in their place, as their substitute. This did not just happen out of the blue. There is a rich Old Testament background to it, where all the blood of all the lambs that were sacrificed throughout all those days was continually pointing forward to *the* blood of *the* Lamb. As a result, the sinner's sin and guilt and punishment has been laid upon the Lord Jesus Christ, instead of being charged to the sinner. In Romans 8:32 we read how God 'did not spare his own Son but delivered him up for us all'.

Christ's blood speaks of his life laid down in death as a sacrifice and offering for sin. God's decree is crystal clear, that 'the soul that sins shall die' (Ezek. 18:4). Equally clear is his affirmation, '"For I have no pleasure in the death of one who dies", says the LORD God. "Therefore turn and live!"' (18:32). Or to state it from the New Testament: 'For the wages of sin is death, but the gift of God is eternal life in Christ Jesus our Lord' (Rom. 6:23). One of the grandest of all the words in the biblical vocabulary of salvation is 'propitiation', which speaks of God turning aside from us (who deserve it) his holy wrath and anger against sin and pouring it out instead upon his spotless Son (who deserves none of it). 'He (Christ) himself is the propitiation for our sins' (1 John 2:2).

So on account of the blood ('the precious blood of Christ, as of a lamb without blemish and without spot', 1 Pet. 1:19) God's wrath and justice in punishing sin is satisfied. The sin is taken away, the guilt cancelled, and the way open for the separation that our sins have caused to be removed, and for us to be reconciled to God, to have peace with him. By God's grace, it is all secured by the blood, for 'without shedding of blood there is no remission' (Heb. 9:22).

(3) *Full salvation*. Is there any sense in Revelation 7:14 of self-salvation or self-deliverance, through the language of *they* washed their robes and *they* made them white? By no means! The provision is God's provision. These ones whom

John sees in heaven have not saved themselves. They could not, and neither can we. There is no such thing as 'do-it-yourself salvation'. 'The eternal praises of the triumphant church will ascribe the salvation of every soul to God and to the Lamb only, to free, sovereign and unmerited grace. In its origin, its execution, its application, its progress, and its final consummation, salvation is of God. It is God's *to save*; it is man's only *to be saved*. The sinner has nothing to do in the whole process, but to receive, and use, and enjoy the free and matchless *grace*'.[6] So what does this manner of language actually indicate?

It speaks of two very important things for our understanding of the way to heaven. The first thing is the sinner's realisation (to which God the Holy Spirit has opened his blind eyes) that there is nothing in the whole of the universe which can wash our sins away and bring us to God except the Saviour's blood, the Saviour's death. 'But now in Christ Jesus you who once were far off have been made near by the blood of Christ' (Eph. 2:13). The second thing is the sinner's casting himself upon Christ, looking solely to Christ, clinging by faith to Christ (even the very faith being 'the gift of God, not of works, lest anyone should boast', Eph. 2:8f), trusting only to Christ and to his blood, his sacrifice, his cross, his death.

> 'His blood can make the foulest clean,
> His blood availed for me'.

The Lamb's blood paid the price for the salvation of those whom John saw. That is the only way it can be. This is the only way to heaven. This is the only way to God. The Lord Jesus Christ himself says, 'I am the way, the truth, and the life. No one comes to the Father except through me' (John

14:6). Peter preached the same fundamental truth of the gospel, with reference to Christ: 'Nor is there salvation in any other, for there is no other name under heaven given among men by which we must be saved' (Acts 4:12).

The uniqueness of Christ and the exclusiveness of the Christian gospel are (shame to say) unpopular emphases these days. Unpopular they may be. But they are true! Would you know the way to heaven, whatever might be popular or unpopular? Here it is. There is only one way. It is the way that God himself has chosen, established and provided in his great grace. It is the way that is opened through his own dear Son, the Lord Jesus Christ, by his blood. You must understand this: no one ever has got or ever will get to heaven any other way. Do not start imagining you will be the first, or the exception that proves the rule!

C H Spurgeon on the way to heaven

Charles Haddon Spurgeon (1834-1892) was born at Kelvedon (Essex) and died at Menton (France). His own moving account of his conversion one snowy January Lord's Day in 1850 in Colchester is well known, and includes these words: 'That happy day, when I found the Saviour, and learned to cling to His dear feet, was a day never to be forgotten by me ... I listened to the Word of God and that precious text led me to the cross of Christ. I can testify that the joy of that day was utterly indescribable. I could have leaped, I could have danced; there was no expression, however fantastical, which would have been out of keeping with the joy of that hour. Many days of Christian experience have passed since then, but there has never been one which has had the full exhilaration, the sparkling delight which that first day had.' The text was Isaiah 45:22 (AV): 'Look unto me, and be ye saved, all the ends of the earth.'

At the age of seventeen he was pastor of the baptist church in the Cambridgeshire village of Waterbeach. In 1854 he was called to New Park Street church in Southwark (London), which congregation later removed to the specially-built Metropolitan Tabernacle in 1861, with regular congregations of around 6,000. Courageously valiant for the truth, the printing of his weekly sermons was commenced in 1855 and continued until 1917, long past his death. The whole enterprise ran to 63 substantial volumes, all still in print today.

It is from one of those sermons on Revelation 7:13-14 (in volume 18, being sermons preached in 1872) that the following extracts are taken.

Drawing out the truth that 'all those in heaven were sinners, for they all needed to wash their robes', he proceeds like this. 'No superfluity would have been written down in this book; but had the robes been perfectly white, there had been no necessity to cleanse them, certainly not to cleanse them in Jesus' blood. They were sinners, then, those glorious ones were sinners like ourselves. Look up at them now! Observe their ravishing beauty! See how faultless they are! And then, remember what they were. Oh, ye trembling sinners, whose bruised hearts dare not indulge a hope of the divine favour, those fair ones were once like you, and you are today what they were once. They were all shapen in iniquity, as you were: they were everyone of them of woman born, and, therefore, conceived in sin. They were all placed in circumstances which allured them to sin; they had their temptations ... and they lived in the midst of an ungodly generation, even as you do. What is more, they all sinned, for mere temptations would not have soiled their robes, but actual sin defiled them. There were thoughts of sin, there were words of sin, there were acts of sin in all of them.'

Coming on to consider the further truth that 'all who are in heaven needed an atonement, and the same atonement as we rely upon', this follows: 'They washed their robes and made them white in the blood of the Lamb. Not one of them became white through his tears of repentance, not one through the shedding of the blood of bulls or of goats. They all wanted a vicarious sacrifice (ie, one in their place), and for none of them was any sacrifice effectual, except the death of Jesus Christ the Lord. They washed their robes nowhere but in the blood of the Lamb. O sinner, that blood of the Lamb is available now. The fountain filled with blood, drawn from Immanuel's veins, is not closed, nor is its efficacy diminished. Every child of Adam now in heaven came there through the blood of the great substitute. This was the key that opened heaven's door – the blood, the blood of the Lamb. It was the one purification of them all, without exception. If I were in thy case, O sinner, God helping me, I would trust in the blood as they did, and enter heaven as they have done.'

A further choice passage in the sermon reads as follows. 'Let us also understand that no amount of sin of which we may have been guilty ought to lead us to despair of pardon, salvation, and ultimate entrance into heaven, if we also wash our robes in the blood of the Lamb. Those who are in heaven have washed their robes white by faith in Jesus, and so may we. I may be addressing someone who has written his own death warrant. I thank God that the Lord has never written it. You may have said, "I know that I shall never have mercy". Who told thee that God had set a limit to his grace? Who has been up to heaven and found that thy name is not written

among his chosen? Oh, do God the justice to believe that he
delighteth in mercy, and that it is one of his greatest joys to
pass by iniquity, transgression, and sin. And, suppose this
day you should have in your own person trouble and sorrow
united; suppose you should be going through the great
tribulation, and at the same time you should have committed
sin which has defiled your garment most conspicuously;
though the gall and the wormwood be both in your cup and
both be bitterest of the bitter, yet do not despair, for the
saints whom John saw had the double blessing of deliverance
and cleansing, and why should not you? I make bold to tell
you that if your troubles were tenfold what they are, and
your sins also were multiplied ten times, yet there is power
in the eternal arm to bear you up under tribulation, and there
is efficacy in the precious blood to remove your sinful stains.
By an act of faith cast yourselves upon God in Christ Jesus.
If you do so, you shall take your place amongst the white-
robed bands when this life ends.'

4

THE BLISS OF HEAVEN

Bliss is a grand old word. It speaks of gladness and enjoyment; of perfect joy and blessedness; of exquisite contentment and the absence of anything to spoil or interfere with that. One of the richest, fullest and most magnificent pictures anywhere in Scripture of the life of the redeemed (God's people) in heaven as a life of bliss is provided in the verses we come to now, continuing straight on in chapter 7, verses 15-17.

We have no photographs, no postcards, no town plans; but in the vision John is given here and that he records for us, we have all that we need to know in order to give us a true idea of life in heaven. The American minister Edward Payson, in a letter to his mother, wrote of how, if he was at home in the early evening, he and his wife would 'sit down and take a little tour up to heaven and see what they are doing there. We try to figure to ourselves how they feel ... and often ... our own feelings become more heavenly; and sometimes God is pleased to open to us a door into heaven, so we get a glimpse of what is transacting there ... and we can scarcely wait till death comes to carry us home'.[7] Oh! that there would be such anticipation and longing in the hearts of all God's children, and that it would stir up to seek the Lord, the God of heaven, any who are reading these lines who are not yet saved.

These three verses reveal, then, a number of features of the bliss of heaven. Let us follow the sequence through carefully.

1 Standing before the throne

Look how verse 15 begins: 'Therefore they are before the throne of God.' 'Therefore' always implies a link, and there is a clear link here with verse 9 and verse 14. There is no doubt as to who they are who 'are before the throne of God'. It must be the same company we have been viewing in verses 13-14. How did they get there? They 'washed their robes and made them white in the blood of the Lamb'. They have been washed clean from sin and made righteous before God through the Lord Jesus Christ, through his death and his blood. As we have already seen, all is of grace to the sinner; all is through Christ for the sinner. As a result of which, here are the redeemed 'before the throne of God'. What a picture of access and welcome it is. They are reconciled to God. They are accepted in his dear Son. They have been fitted for heaven to live with him there.

The word 'before' is especially noteworthy. It speaks of fellowship with God in his immediate presence. It is not something at a distance, round the corner, next door, on the outskirts of heaven, or out of sight. 'Before the throne' means before the Lord, in the very presence of the one, true and living God – even in that numberless throng! Our whole life in heaven will be 'before the throne of God'. It will not be a static, inactive or uneventful life, but it will be continually and consciously in his presence; fully and intimately so. We are reminded of Paul's words: 'absent from the body and ... present with the Lord' (2 Cor. 5:8). Can you imagine it?

2 Serving God in his temple

At the beginning of our studies we observed that heaven is the dwelling place of God. Now it is described as God's 'temple', and those who are in heaven with him, standing before his throne, 'serve him day and night in his temple'.

The word used here for 'temple' means inner shrine or sanctuary, and corresponds to the holy of holies in the wilderness tabernacle and the Jerusalem temple of Old Testament days. The idea is this: the place where God dwells, where the Most High has his abode, the sanctuary of his holiness, the place where he is worshipped and adored. Do not imagine that there is any contradiction with John's statement in 21:22, 'I saw no temple in it, for the Lord God Almighty and the Lamb are its temple.' The way we might put it (conscious of our great limitation of language and expression) is to say there will be no 'going to church' in heaven. The whole of heaven is God's temple, not just some part of it or some area within it. Wherever in the eternity of heaven we turn, wherever we look, wherever we go, we shall know his presence. All the redeemed and all the redeemed creation will walk before him, worship him and serve him to his glory. Then (at last!) we shall glorify God and enjoy him for ever.

Back in 1:6 we are told that the Lord Jesus Christ, in all his work on our behalf, 'has made us kings and priests to his God and Father'. Our priestly service which begins here, worshipping and serving the living God, will come to full and perfect fruition in heaven.

Also of striking importance is the phrase 'day and night'. Again there is no contradiction within Revelation, when we learn 'there shall be no night there' (22:5). 'Day and night' in 7:15 means without ceasing. Indeed it not only means that; it also means without weariness, without weakness, without staleness, without distraction. Here on earth our 'best' worship and our 'best' service (if we may so speak) is always tainted with so many imperfections, wanderings, coldnesses and such like. Our bodies are frail, our minds are distracted, our hearts are divided. We are forever up and down, keen and careless, fruitful and barren. How very little do we really worship God 'in spirit and truth' (John 4:24). Time and again we have to seek God's pardon for the sheer poverty of what we have rendered to him. But not in heaven! Our worship of God in his temple will not be subject to any of the hindrances which clog it and defile it here on earth.

The remarkable chapters which close the prophecy of Ezekiel build up to this final climax: 'The LORD is there' (Ezek. 48:35). As we view the bliss of heaven through our verses in Revelation 7, this is the glory of that bliss, surely: the Lord is there. His holy, majestic and all-gracious presence pervades the whole of the place. 'By his triumphant ascension our great High Priest, the incarnate Son who is both our sacrificial Lamb and our risen Lord, not only himself entered into the heavenly sanctuary but also opened the way for us into that true holy of holies, which is the glorious presence of God.'[8]

3 Covered by God's tent

Both the AV and NKJV translate here that the one who sits on the throne will 'dwell among them'. However, we would do better on this occasion to follow the NIV which captures the sense of the original with 'he who sits on the throne will spread his tent over them'. The picture of God's tent, or covering, is to the fore here. It speaks very welcomingly and beautifully of the warmth of God's love, the security of his protection and the tenderness of his care.

In this respect it is very reminiscent of those exquisite Old Testament pictures of taking refuge under God's wings and him covering us with his feathers. Here are two choice samples. The words of Boaz to Ruth: 'The LORD repay your work, and a full reward be given you by the LORD God of Israel, under whose wings you have come for refuge' (Ruth 2:12). The assurance testified to by the psalmist: 'He who dwells in the secret place of the Most High shall abide under the shadow of the Almighty ... He shall cover you with his feathers, and under his wings you shall take refuge' (Ps. 91:1, 4). We could add, from the New Testament, the words of the Lord Jesus Christ in his lament over Jerusalem: 'O Jerusalem, Jerusalem, the one who kills the prophets and stones those who are sent to her! How often I wanted to gather your children together, as a hen gathers her chicks under her wings, but you were not willing!' (Matt. 23:37).

While meditating upon this delightful theme, several other Scripture verses come to mind. 'He brought me to the banqueting house, and his banner over me was love' is the happy testimony of the bride as she reflects upon how her beloved has dealt in love with her, speaking of the believer's and the church's experience of the love of Christ, our heavenly bridegroom (Song 2:4). 'You will show me the path of life; in your presence is fullness of joy; at your right hand are pleasures for evermore' (Ps. 16:11).

Finally, there is the promise of God given in Ezekiel 37:26-28: 'Moreover I will make a covenant of peace with them, and it shall be an everlasting covenant with them: I will establish them and multiply them, and I will set my sanctuary in their midst for evermore. My tabernacle also shall be with them; indeed I will be their God, and they shall be my people. The nations also will know that I, the LORD, sanctify Israel, when my sanctuary is in their midst for evermore.'

It is always profitable to trace through the Scriptures various connections which, side by side, open up precious themes
and doctrines, thereby reminding us that the whole of God's
Word is a wonderful unity.

4 Enjoying God's provision

This takes us into verse 16, with its lovely promise, 'They
shall neither hunger nor thirst anymore.' I have written elsewhere upon these words that 'we shall have everything we
desire and desire everything we have'.[9] So we shall.

That contrasts very much with this life, we must admit.
Here we sometimes desire things (whether right things or
wrong things) that we do not have; and we do not always
desire, regard or appreciate many good things with which
God has blessed us. How different will heaven be! There
will be no want, no lack, nothing missing, nothing forgotten or overlooked. It is not that we shall have no desires or
needs. Rather, we shall enjoy God's never-failing supply.
There will be no unfulfilled desire, no necessity, no anxi-
ety, no concerns. Most importantly of all, our hunger and
thirst after God himself, after the Lord Jesus Christ, after
the Holy Spirit, after righteousness will be fully satisfied.
Hunger and thirst are classic expressions of desperate need.
All that, however, will be past. It will belong to the days on
earth. The Saviour's luscious promise of Matthew 5:6 will
be completely fulfilled: 'Blessed are those who hunger and
thirst for righteousness, for they shall be filled.' The psalmist's holy confidence will be entirely realised: 'As for me, I
will see your face in righteousness; I shall be satisfied when
I awake in your likeness' (Ps. 17:15). Indeed, heaven will
exceed all our desires.

We can work this out a little like this. Our bodies will be

glorified and perfected. Our sins will have gone for ever. Our enemies will have been all destroyed. Our hearts will be fixed upon him in whose divine presence we dwell. Our company and fellowship will be with God and his people. Our eyes will see the King in his beauty and will gaze upon him whom our souls love. As one has put it: 'To be supplied when we hunger is the mercy of earth: never to hunger at all is the plenitude of heaven'.[10]

5 Kept by God's power

While journeying through this life we are surrounded by 'many dangers, toils and snares'. Such are pictured in the second part of verse 16 by the sun and the scorching heat, and the promise is this as part of the bliss of heaven: 'the sun will not strike them, nor any heat.'

Sometimes, especially in cold or wet weather when our spirits feel as chill and damp within as the weather outside, we long for some sunshine. But you can get too much of the sun. It can cause sunburn, sunstroke, and even (we are told) skin cancer and death. So what does verse 16b teach us?

Let Scripture interpret Scripture (which is always the best and safest way). 'They shall not hurt or destroy in all my holy mountain' (Isa. 11:9). Trials, tribulations, dangers and all the problems arising from sin and Satan will be unknown in heaven. Glance back to verse 14 and God's people coming 'out of the great tribulation'. Emphasise the 'out of'. Nothing will come near us – ever – to cause us any harm. All the disharmonies of nature and all the pollutions of the environment will have gone. Nothing within us and nothing outside us will be there to trouble us.

There will be no more suffering for the precious name

of the Lord Jesus Christ. Here on earth, 'all who desire to lead a godly life in Christ Jesus will suffer persecution' (2 Tim. 3:12) – but not in heaven. We shall no more be hindered or held back by these fragile bodies that we inhabit. What will beat upon us, or shine upon us, will be the glory of the Lord – that the full sight of which we could not at present bear. In heaven, though, it will neither consume us with its heat nor blind us with its dazzling power.

We must not miss, from these verses, the way in which one thing leads to another and one thing follows another. It is precisely because the glorified people of God abide under his shadow and dwell under his tent that the promises of both parts of verse 16 apply. That is what guarantees it to be so. What an abiding place that will be! What a joy it must be in heaven – we can scarcely begin to imagine it at the moment! – to be forever within the circle of God's eternal presence.

'In heaven they (the glorified) are able to endure the immediate presence of God, not only because of the Mediatorship of Christ, through whom the glory of God shines with tempered splendour upon the saints, but also because they themselves are strengthened. From all this earthly grossness quit, they are enabled to stand in that light to which no mortal man can now approach. To us even "our God is a consuming fire" while we are here; but in the saints there remaineth nothing to consume. The light of God is not too bright for eyes that Christ hath touched with heaven's own eye-salve. The vision of the Infinite is not too glorious for those whom the Lord has prepared to be with him and to see his face. What John of Patmos could bear, the weakest saint in heaven can endure, not for an hour, but for the whole stretch of eternity.'

6 Shepherded by the Lamb

We come to verse 17, and what a glorious verse it is – one to do our needy souls good. You may remember those lines of Anne Ross Cousin, drawn from words of Samuel Rutherford: 'The Lamb is all the glory of Immanuel's land.' So he is; 'for the Lamb who is in the midst of the throne will shepherd them and lead them to living fountains of waters.'

Wait a moment, though. Is there not something strange here, something which does not quite go together? We read that 'the Lamb ... will shepherd them' (NIV, 'the Lamb ... will be their shepherd'). Both titles, Lamb and Shepherd, belong to the Lord Jesus Christ, our glorious Saviour and Head. But how can he who is 'the Lamb' be also 'the Shepherd'? Surely a lamb is a lamb, and a shepherd is a shepherd. A lamb is not a shepherd as well, neither is a shepherd a lamb. Is he? Ordinarily not; but in this unique case: yes!

Our Lord Jesus Christ, heaven's beloved one, God's dear Son, the best beloved of our souls, is the Lamb and the Shepherd. Spurgeon remarks, 'A lamb is a member of the flock; but in this case the Lamb is the shepherd of the flock: a shepherd who is also a lamb must be the most tender shepherd conceivable; the most sympathetic and brotherly guardian that can be.' Moreover, he 'is in the midst of the throne'. He has become the centre of all things. Everything revolves around him.

Here is Spurgeon again. Savour these words carefully. 'Think of that, the lamb in the midst of the throne. Can you put these two things together, a sacrifice and a throne? That same Saviour who opened his veins that he might cleanse us from sin now wears the imperial purple of the universe. He that stooped to be made sin for us is now supreme sovereign, King of kings and Lord of lords. Think of that and be

comforted. Our Representative is glorified. Our covenant
Head, our second Adam, is in the midst of the throne. God
the Father hath exalted the Mediator to the place of power
and honour and rule. Our Saviour hath all power in heaven
and in earth. Sometimes when I think of my great King and
Captain exalted to so glorious an estate, I feel that it matters nothing what becomes of me, his poor follower. The
sun of persecution smites not when he is seen as God over
all, blessed for ever. Hunger is not hunger, and pain is not
pain, for such a loved one. In blissful sympathy with the
unutterable delights of Jesus, we are happy at our worst,
feeling that if Christ be rich we are not poor, and if Christ
be happy we are not disappointed. His victory is our victory. His glory is our glory. Feel this union with your en-
throned Lord, and you will begin to be in heaven.'

He is the Lamb. John the Baptist was very clear about
this, and announced it boldly and gladly for all to hear.
'Behold! The Lamb of God, who takes away the sin of the
world!' (John 1:29). Or recall verse 14 of our present chapter,
Revelation 7, where this same title is used of the Saviour in
connection with his sacrificial and atoning blood.

He is the Shepherd. In the course of the New Testament,
the Lord Jesus Christ is set forth as 'the good shepherd',
the 'great shepherd' and 'the chief shepherd'. In his own
words he declares, 'I am the good shepherd. The good shepherd gives his life for the sheep' (John 10:11). We also read
of him: 'Now may the God of peace who brought up our
Lord Jesus from the dead, that great shepherd of the sheep,
through the blood of the everlasting covenant ...' (Heb.
13:20); and, 'when the chief shepherd appears, you will
receive the crown of glory that does not fade away' (1 Pet.
5:4). In particular, in our present reference, the name 'shep-

herd' pictures his tender pastoral care for his flock. For
Old Testament demonstrations of the same, observe Psalm
23:1, Isaiah 40:11 and Micah 5:4.

Wonder of wonders! In heaven's glory the Lord Jesus
Christ will be to us both the Lamb (through whom we have
eternal salvation) and the Shepherd (who looks after us for
ever). How does he do so? By leading us 'to living fountains
of waters' (literally, 'fountains of waters of life'). Consistently in Scripture water symbolises salvation and eternal
life. Just think of such choice texts as these. 'Therefore with
joy you will draw water from the wells of salvation' (Isa.
12:3). 'Ho! Everyone who thirsts, come to the waters' (Isa.
55:1). 'Whoever drinks of this water will thirst again, but
whoever drinks of the water I shall give him will never thirst.
But the water that I shall give him will become in him a
fountain of water springing up into everlasting life' (John
4:13f). 'On the last day, that great day of the feast, Jesus
stood and cried out, saying, "If anyone thirsts, let him come
to me and drink. He who believes in me, as the Scripture
has said, out of his heart will flow rivers of living water"'
(John 7:37f). 'And let him who thirsts come. And whoever
desires, let him take the water of life freely' (Rev. 22:17).

So verse 17 teaches us that our Shepherd will feed us,
tend us, refresh us and supply all our needs. He will minister to us of himself. We shall be at the very source of spiritual life and blessing. There will be nothing borrowed or
second-hand about our experience of Christ in heaven, or
about our enjoyment of him. We shall drink directly from
the spring! Of he who is himself the fountain of life, we
may say, 'All our springs are in him!' All of which underscores a very important aspect of the bliss of heaven. It will
never cease to satisfy. It will never grow stale. 'Nothing

refreshes the imagination more than smiling meadows, purl-
ing streams, murmuring brooks and pleasant cascades; and
therefore the Saviour is said to lead His people into living
fountains of water'.[11] Hence the language of Scripture here.
The picture of our Lamb-Shepherd leading us 'to living
fountains of waters' has the sure sense of him continually
showing fresh delights to his redeemed and glorified flock,
such that even in heaven (far from us having arrived and
'that being it') he will be leading us on and on, deeper and
deeper, higher and higher in spiritual ecstasies that we cannot yet even begin to imagine. Even in heaven we shall be
going from glory to glory. Our God and Saviour is inexhaustible! Our present scanty thought will forever be being
enlarged with ever-expanding views of our Lord Jesus
Christ. Gone for ever will be our dark seasons, our spiritual
desertions, our cries of 'Oh, that I knew where I might find
him' (Job 23:3) or 'Have you seen the one I love?' (Song
3:3). No more withdrawings of his face!

7 Comforted by the Lord

What can you say about the end of verse 17? 'And God will
wipe away every tear from their eyes.' This is not the first
time in the Bible that we are given such a promise. It is
there, for example, way back in Isaiah 25:8: 'And the LORD
God will wipe away tears from all faces.' Here is God's
remarkable personal touch combining his divine power and
his divine compassion. The bliss of heaven includes even
this: every cause of sorrow and suffering will be excluded,
such that our tears will have been wiped not only 'from'
but (quite literally) 'out of' our eyes.

For a fuller picture and explanation of this, consider
21:3f: 'And I heard a loud voice from heaven saying,

"Behold, the tabernacle of God is with men, and he will dwell with them, and they shall be his people, and God himself will be with them and be their God. And God will wipe away every tear from their eyes; there shall be no more death, nor sorrow, nor crying; and there shall be no more pain, for the former things have passed away."' Notice that: 'for the former things have passed away.' And lest this all appears too good to be true, read on to the next verse: 'Then he who sat on the throne said, "Behold, I make all things new." And he said to me, "Write, for these words are true and faithful."' Notice that: God makes 'all things new'.

Should this still be a matter of amazement, such that you wonder just how it can be, remember what lies behind it all: 'And there shall be no more curse' (22:3). All the curse that fallen Adam brought upon himself and all the earth ('just as through one man sin entered the world, and death through sin, and thus death spread to all men, because all sinned', Rom. 5:12) will have completely gone, been taken away, removed, erased, undone.

> Where He displays His healing power,
> Death and the curse are known no more;
> In Him the tribes of Adam boast
> More blessings than their father lost
>
> Isaac Watts

The 'in him', of course, in the third line, is a reference to the Lord Jesus Christ. 'For if by the one man's offence many died, much more the grace of God and the gift by the grace of the one man, Jesus Christ, abounded to many.... For as by one man's disobedience many were made sinners, so also by one man's obedience many will be made righteous' (Rom. 5:15,19).

It is not only a matter of what our God delivers us out of

(sin, death, the curse, hell, and so on), but of what he delivers us in to as well – the bliss of heaven! Have you grasped this? Do you have a clear sense of what this bliss excludes and of what it includes? Do you bless God and give him all the glory for it? Do you live every day of your Christian life in anticipation of the prospect of it, while, even now, you are pressing on to know Christ? Is your present Christian life, seeking to live near to God, a sort of 'rough draft' of the life of full communion with God that you look forward to above?

And (tying in with what we discovered in the earlier chapters on the purity of heaven and the way to heaven) do you see how it is so utterly impossible for anyone to go to heaven except through the Lord Jesus Christ? Let me write in a personal manner for a moment: how can you think of taking delight in Christ then if you do not take delight in him now? How could he be your Lamb and Shepherd there if he is not your Lamb and Shepherd here? It is never enough merely to hope that you will go to heaven. You need to know that you will, otherwise your hope will be a miserable, dashed and disappointed thing. And you can only know that you are going to heaven if you are relying entirely and exclusively upon the Lord Jesus Christ – his obedient life, his sin-bearing death, his character as the spotless and righteous one who is the sinner's Substitute and Saviour.

J C Ryle on the bliss of heaven

John Charles Ryle (1816-1900) has been described as 'that man of granite, with the heart of a child'. A man of great height (he measured nearly six feet four) and, says one, 'strong as a horse', he was a clergyman of the Church of England, and is best known as the first bishop of Liverpool (although before his twenty years in that role, he had ministered in country parishes for 39 years). He died at the age of 83, having been converted when he was 21. He records these words in his *Autobiography*, when looking back to the time of his conversion: 'Nothing I can remember to this day appeared to me so clear and distinct as my own sinfulness, Christ's preciousness, the value of the Bible, the absolute necessity of coming out of the world, the need of being born again.... Before that time I was dead in sins and on the high road to hell, and from that time I have become alive and had a hope of heaven. And nothing to my mind can account for it, but the free sovereign grace of God.'

A stalwart for the faith, valiant for the truth, many of his writings are still in print, and both widely and profitably read. Foremost among them are classics like *Holiness* and his volumes of *Expository Thoughts on the Gospels*. A lesser known volume is *The Christian Race* (originally published in 1900) – a collection of sermons including one on Revelation 7:14-17, entitled *The Blood of the Lamb*. It is from this that the following two extracts are taken.

With respect to what is written in verse 17, he asks, 'But what is the crowning privilege?', and continues as follows. 'The Lord Jesus Christ Himself shall minister to their comforts; the same kind hand which raised them from the death of sin to the life of righteousness, which healed their spiritual diseases, and brought them health and peace, and made them new creatures upon earth, the same hand shall welcome them in heaven, and conduct them as highly favoured guests to a banquet of happiness, such as eye hath not seen, neither can it enter into the heart of man to conceive. Time was when He sought them out as wandering sheep in the wilderness of this world, and made them members of

His little flock by the renewing of the Holy Ghost, and refreshed their weary, heavy laden souls with the water of life. And the same Jesus who began the good work in the days of their tribulation upon earth, the same Good Shepherd shall complete the work in heaven. Here they have tasted something of the streams, a little trembling company, from north and south, east and west, but there they will be gathered round the fountain itself, and there will be one fold and one shepherd, one heart and one mind, and none shall make them afraid.

And then there will be no more weeping, for "God Himself shall wipe away all tears". A dwelling-place in which there will be no more weeping! I know no part of heaven more difficult to imagine. We live in a world of sorrow, a very vale of tears; tears for ourselves and tears for others, tears over our own shortcomings, tears over the unbelief of those we love, tears over disappointed hopes, tears over the graves of those on whom our affections are set, and all because of sin: there would have been no sorrow if Adam had never fallen, but our very weeping is a proof of sin.

Yet it shall not always be so: a day is still to come when sadness shall flee away, and God Himself shall say, Refrain thy voice from weeping, for the former things are passed away. There shall be no sadness in heaven, for there shall be no sin; the days of our tribulation shall be forgotten; we shall be able at last to love our God without coldness, to reverence His holiness without torment, to trust Him without despair, to serve Him without weariness, without interruption, without distraction; the days of weakness and corruption will be past, and we shall be like unto our Lord in holiness as well as happiness, in purity as well as immortality.'

He concludes the sermon in this manner. 'But blessed are all ye that mourn, for ye shall be comforted; blessed are ye that are persecuted for righteousness' sake, for great is your reward in heaven. Ye have wept with them that weep, but ye shall soon rejoice with them that rejoice, and your joy shall no man take away. It is but a single step, and you shall be for ever with the Lord, where the wicked cease from troubling, and the weary are at rest. The worm may destroy these bodies, and yet in the flesh shall ye see God, and your own eyes shall behold Him, and your own ears shall hear Him say, "Come, ye blessed of my Father, inherit the kingdom prepared for you from the foundation of the world." The saints whose faith and patience you have so often admired; the holy men and women of whom you have so often said, "Oh, that I were like them"; the ministers who have shown you the way of life, and implored you to be steadfast and unmoveable; the friends who advised you to come out of the world, and took sweet counsel with you about the kingdom of God; the beloved ones of your own house, who slept in Jesus and went home before you: all are there, all waiting to receive you, and there shall be no more parting, no more weeping, no more separation; and you, even you, this vile body being changed, shall sing the song of the redeemed: "Unto Him that loved us, and washed us from our sins in His own blood, and hath made us kings and priests unto God and His Father, to Him be glory and dominion for ever and ever."

In this world ye may have tribulation, but be of good cheer: your Lord and Saviour hath overcome the world.'

5

THE VISION OF HEAVEN

Are you familiar with the phrase 'the beatific vision'? Do you know what it means? It is something very special upon which Scripture has much to say.

Job spoke of it and looked forward to it. 'For I know that my Redeemer lives, and he shall stand at last on the earth; and after my skin is destroyed, this I know, that in my flesh I shall see God, whom I shall see for myself, and my eyes shall behold, and not another. How my heart yearns within me!' (Job 19:25-27).

So did *David*. 'As for me, I will see your face in righteousness; I shall be satisfied when I awake in your likeness' (Ps. 17:15).

Isaiah was sure of it. 'Your eyes will see the King in his beauty; they will see the land that is very far off' (Isa. 33:17).

The apostle *Paul* had it much in mind, upon one interpretation of 1 Corinthians 13:12. 'For now we see in a mirror, dimly, but then face to face. Now I know in part, but then I shall know just as I also am known.'

So did the apostle *John*. 'Beloved, now we are children of God; and it has not yet been revealed what we shall be, but we know that when he is revealed, we shall be like him, for we shall see him as he is' (1 John 3:2).

So also, we might say, by implication, did the apostle *Peter*. Speaking of the Lord Jesus Christ, he writes, 'whom having not seen you love. Though now you do not see him, yet believing, you rejoice with joy inexpressible and full of glory' (1 Pet. 1:8).

The *writer to the Hebrews* is not left out. 'Pursue peace with all men, and holiness, without which no one will see the Lord' (Heb. 12:14).

Most importantly of all, *the Lord Jesus Christ* himself has this to say in the course of the Beatitudes at the commencement of his Sermon on the Mount. 'Blessed are the pure in heart, for they shall see God' (Matt. 5:8).

Enough clues should by now have been given, if you needed them, to indicate what is meant by 'the beatific vision'. It is the sight of God in heaven. This is *the* vision of heaven. We shall see *him*. We shall gaze upon *him*. We shall be taken up supremely with *him*.

Someone might want to interject and say, 'But what of a verse of Scripture like Exodus 33:20, where God says to Moses, "You cannot see my face; for no man shall see me, and live."' The thing is that such an impossibility (of seeing God's face and still being alive rather than utterly consumed by the sight) is true only of mortals. It does not apply when we have 'put on immortality' (1 Cor. 15:53). True enough, were we to be admitted to such a sight at present, our souls and bodies would not be able to bear it. We would be overpowered, if not destroyed. But in the glory-land of heaven, to see God's face will be the very 'essence and excellence' of our life. Thomas Watson describes the sight of God as 'the heaven of heaven'. So does Spurgeon, and he also refers to it as 'the cream of heaven'. We think about it all too little, and (inevitably) we understand it and grasp it all too poorly; but what a magnificent theme it is!

> How wonderful, how beautiful,
> The sight of Thee must be,
> Thine endless wisdom, boundless power,
> And aweful purity!   F W Faber

The point at which the beatific vision is in greatest prominence in the book of Revelation is 22:4. We have already observed, in an earlier chapter, that chapter 21 is full of symbols and pictures which add up to a description of the blessedness of the life of the glorified church when gathered into heaven with Christ. The same is true of much of chapter 22, the last chapter of the book and the closing chapter of the Bible – God's last word. There is a strong sense of 'the best is yet to be'. This final chapter features a picture of heaven as a garden. There is a garden at the beginning of the Bible, which turns into paradise lost, and there is a garden at the end of the Bible, which sets forth paradise regained and restored. 'A pure river of the water of life, clear as crystal, proceeding from the throne of God and of the Lamb' flows through the garden. There is 'the tree of life' with its fruit. There is the assurance of the removal of the curse.

At the very heart of the revelation given to John here is this amazing statement: 'They shall see his face' (v. 4). That is the beatific vision! The word 'beatific' (compare 'beatitudes') speaks of blessedness. It is the blessed vision. For beholding God's face we shall be at the very fount and height of blessedness. All the veil will be removed and God will show himself to us in all his glory, just as a king on his coronation day shows himself in all his royalty and splendour.

The word 'face', of course, is a manner of speaking. What is indicated thereby is the presence of God, the glory of God, the nearness of God, the fellowship of God, the enjoyment of God. It reminds us that fundamental to this beatific vision will be our sight of the risen, ascended and glorified Lord Jesus Christ, through whom the divine beams of God's glory, wisdom, holiness, majesty, mercy and love will shine forth most brightly upon our souls. You cannot help thinking of these words of the Saviour: 'And this is eternal life, that they may know you, the only true God, and Jesus Christ whom you have sent' (John 17:3). Even then, though, you must remember, God remains unfathomable. As someone has remarked, 'We shall understand God to the limit of our capacities, just as he knows us according to his infinite capacity.'

There is so much that we just cannot say about the vision of God, precisely because it is the vision of God, and we do not know. Ultimately, we shall have to wait and see. Yet even though we cannot understand all of the matter, we may still rejoice in it; and even though so much of it presently remains hidden from us, it is still a most glorious theme to explore. In fact, there are certain things we can say about it with biblical confidence, and it would be profitable to consider such under the headings of present and future.

The present beginning of the beatific vision: in this life
Although 22:4 is cast in the future ('They *shall see* his face'), there is something strongly of the present bound up in it, and very importantly so. What do I mean? If you are a Christian, if you have experienced the new birth and conversion, then even now your eyes have been opened, your blindness has been taken away, and something of the veil has been removed so that with the eye of faith you see God. It is worth working this out a little.

You see him in *his world*, for all his works praise him and his divine and perfect signature is written upon all that he has made. 'The heavens declare the glory of God; and the firmament shows his handiwork. Day unto day utters speech, and night unto night reveals knowledge' (Ps. 19:1-2). 'For since the creation of the world his invisible attributes are clearly seen, being understood by the things that are made, even his eternal power and Godhead, so that they are without excuse' (Rom. 1:20). As it has been put poetically:

> Heaven above is softer blue,
>   Earth around is sweeter green;
> Something lives in every hue
>   Christless eyes have never seen:
> Birds with gladder songs o'erflow,
>   Flowers with deeper beauties shine,
> Since I know, as now I know,
>   I am His and He is mine.
>
> G W Robinson.

You see him in *his Word*, for he is to be found revealing himself upon every page to those who have been given eyes to see. The Bible is 'the word of God which lives and abides for ever' (1 Pet. 1:23), just as he himself lives and abides for ever. 'All Scripture is given by inspiration of God' (2 Tim. 3:16). 'The entrance of your words gives light' (Ps. 119:130). Or remember that occasion when the Lord Jesus Christ, in speaking to the Jews, said 'You search the Scriptures, for in them you think you have eternal life; and these are they which testify of me' (John 5:39). Which leads us to this:

You see him in *his Son*, the Lord Jesus Christ, of whom the Father testifies on more than one occasion, 'This is my beloved Son, in whom I am well pleased. Hear him!' (eg. Matt. 17:5). A number of Scriptures bear significantly upon this. 'No one has seen God at any time. The only begotten Son, who is in the bosom of the Father, he has declared him' (John 1:18). 'For it is the God who commanded light to shine out of darkness who has shone in our hearts to give the light of the knowledge of the glory of God in the face of Jesus Christ' (2 Cor. 4:6). The writer to the Hebrews speaks of the Lord Jesus Christ 'being the brightness of his [God's] glory and the express image of his person' (Heb. 1:3), while the Son himself confesses, 'He who has seen me has seen the Father' (John 14:9).

You see him in *his grace*, which he has lavished upon us poor vile sinners, reconciling us to himself through the blood of his Son, bringing us near when once we were far off, adopting us into his family as rescued and redeemed and much-loved children when once we were outcasts and no people at all. All of this (and much more!) is 'to the praise of the glory of his grace, by which he has made us accepted in the Beloved' (Eph. 1:6).

You see him in *his ordinances or sacraments*, as baptism testifies to the wonders of God's covenant grace and our union with Christ, and as in the Lord's supper we 'proclaim the Lord's death until he comes' (1 Cor. 11:26; compare 10:16).

You see him in *his providences*. There is a magnificent statement with respect to providence in section 5 of the Westminster Confession of Faith. 'God the great Creator of all things doth uphold, direct, dispose, and govern all creatures, actions, and things, from the greatest even to the least, by his most wise and holy providence, according to his infallible foreknowledge, and the free and immutable counsel of his own will, to the praise of the glory of his wisdom, power, justice, goodness, and mercy.' And again: 'As the providence of God doth in general reach to all creatures, so after a most special manner it taketh care of his Church, and disposeth all things to the good thereof.' The psalmist

David brings it right home to our own door and our own heart when he says, 'I will cry out to God Most High, to God who performs all things for me' (Ps. 57:2). What does our God do for us in his providence? Let the apostle Paul reply. 'And we know that all things work together for good to those who love God, to those who are the called according to his purpose' (Rom. 8:28).

You see him *in history*, as he governs all the affairs of men and nations, even turning the wrath of man to his praise. 'The Lord reigns' (Ps. 93:1). 'But the Lord is in his holy temple. Let all the earth keep silence before him' (Hab. 2:20).

And you see him at *his throne*, where he has given us the right, as his children, to go in to see him at any time in the blessed name of the Lord Jesus Christ, his dear Son and our dear Saviour. We have 'received the Spirit of adoption by whom we cry out "Abba, Father"' (Rom. 8:15), and are both invited and commanded to 'come boldly to the throne of grace, that we may obtain mercy and find grace to help in time of need' (Heb. 4:16).

It must be acknowledged, of course, that all of this seeing God in our present life is 'by faith, not by sight' (2 Cor. 5:7), but that does not make it any less real. How are we told that Moses endured? It was 'as seeing him who is invisible' (Heb. 11:27). He could not see God with the eyes of sight, any more than we can; but he could and did see God with the eyes of faith, and so can we.

The future blessedness of the beatific vision: in the life to come

Let me ask you: what would you say will be your ultimate blessedness and happiness in glory? Will it be being reunited with loved ones who died in the Lord? Will it be seeing old and dear Christian friends again? Will it be meeting the heroes of Scripture and of church history for the first time? Will it be that you will no longer have to struggle with sin, battle with sickness or be cast down with sorrow, and that you will no longer grieve God in any way? The truth is that it will be none of these things, precious though each one admittedly is and will be.

Our present verse from Revelation gives us the ultimate, highest, richest blessedness of the children of God: 'they shall see his face.' The view, the sight, the vision of God himself will be the chief thing. It will outshine everything else. This is the glory of glories. The glory of heaven itself will be glorious enough (just think – if you can! – what heaven itself will be like, how it will appear). Then there will be the glory of the angels as well as the glory of the saints and their fellowship with one another. But the glory that excelleth is this: the vision of God, the beatific vision, seeing God's face. Thomas Brooks has this to say. 'As the best rest, so the best sight and knowledge of God is reserved for believers till they come to heaven. I readily grant that even in this world the saints do know the Lord, inwardly, spiritually, powerfully, feelingly, experimentally, transformingly, practically; but yet, notwithstanding all this, the best knowledge of God is reserved for heaven.'[12]

'Oh, brethren, if communion with God on earth be so sweet, if the presence of God in means and ordinances be so precious, if one day in his courts is better than a thousand, what will an eternity in his immediate presence be? ... And if the vision on "the holy mount" was so sweet, if the attractions of that moment were so ravishing that Peter said, "It is good for us to be here", what shall it be to behold the countless unfoldings of this glory throughout eternity?'[13]

Given the grandeur and mystery of all this, can we say anything about it at all? Let us try. This vision of God will be *an all-surpassing sight*. We may be absolutely sure that it will be beyond anything and everything we have ever seen or thought or known before of our God. If it has been a blessed thing to behold something of God (not least in the face of the Lord Jesus Christ) here, what will it be like there? If he has given us at times such gracious and remarkable views of himself from a distance, so to speak, what will the sight be like when we are face to face?

The vision of God will be *a transforming sight*. We shall ourselves be transformed with the view. We shall be changed. Concerning the Lord Jesus, the apostle John declares, 'we shall be like him, for we shall see him as he is' (1 John 3:2). In heaven, the saints will so see God as to be changed into his image, at last to be holy. The oft-meditated upon promise of 2 Corinthians 3:18 will actually have come true. It will have materialised. 'But we all, with unveiled face, beholding as in a mirror the glory of the Lord, are being transformed into the same image from glory to glory, just as by the Spirit of the Lord.'

Without any doubt, the vision of God will be *a joyful and gladdening sight*. Surely it must be that! How could it ever be otherwise? What is there to be found in his presence? Fulness of joy. What is awaiting us at his right hand? Pleasures for evermore. So says the psalmist (Ps. 16:11). If we may know (on all-too-rare occasions) even now 'joy inexpressible and full of glory' (1 Pet. 1:8), what shall we experience then, do you imagine? Listen to Thomas Watson: 'If the joy of faith be such, what will the joy of vision be? The sight of Christ will amaze the eye with wonder and ravish the heart with joy. If the face of a friend whom we entirely love so affects us and drives away sorrow, O how cheering will the sight of God be to the saints in heaven! Then indeed it may be said, "Your heart shall rejoice" (John 16:22).'[14]

There is more. The vision of God will be a *fulfilling sight*. It is Watson again who captures the thought exactly when he remarks that 'the sight of God satisfies'. Was not this the psalmist's testimony and assurance (Ps. 17:15)? Only he can satisfy us in this vale of tears, and he, most assuredly, will satisfy us in that land of joy. There are shades here of Ephesians 3:18-19, being 'able to comprehend with all the saints what is the width and length and depth and height – to know the love of Christ which passes knowledge; that you may be filled with all the fulness of God.'

Certainly the vision of God will be *a comforting sight*. How exquisitely we are assured of this in a verse like Isaiah 35:10: 'And the ransomed of the LORD shall return, and come to Zion with singing, with everlasting joy on their heads. They shall obtain joy and gladness, and sorrow and sighing shall flee away.' You have the very same in Isaiah 51:11. It is worth recording twice! Death is no threat to the Christian. It takes us to Christ and to heavenly comforts. The night will have gone, and the day will have dawned. Remember how this is promised back in Proverbs 4:18: 'But the path of the just is like the shining sun (light), that shines ever brighter unto the perfect day.' 'The thoughts of this beatifical vision should carry a Christian full sail with joy through the waters of affliction' (Thomas Watson again). What a lifting up for the downcast the prospect of the beatific vision should be.

So shall His presence bless our souls,
And shed a joyful light;
That hallowed morn shall chase away
The sorrows of the night.

                                        Scottish Paraphrases.

This gives rise to a further thought. The vision of God will be *an immediate sight*. The apostle Paul was confident of this. 'For to me, to live is Christ, and to die is gain' (Phil. 1:21). The twice repeated verb 'is' in our English versions is not there in Paul's original. We supply it for the sake of grammar. What he literally said was as crisp and direct as this: 'for to me, to live Christ, and to die gain.' What was life for Paul? Christ: trusting him, knowing him, loving him, serving him, enjoying him, being made like him, and so on. And what was death for Paul? In a word, gain. Why gain? In verse 23 of the same first chapter of Philippians he tells us: 'having a desire to depart and be with Christ, which is far better.' Again our English version has to supply the verb, for what Paul wrote literally was just this: 'having the desire to depart and be with Christ, for by much rather better.' He was certain of this.

Something similar, of course, comes through in what he writes in 2 Corinthians 5:8 where we read this: 'We are confident, yes, well pleased rather to be absent from the body and to be present with the Lord.' Hence the immediacy of the sight of God for the believer. We shall see him straightaway upon death, as we enter immediately into his holy and heavenly presence. There is no waiting or delaying. So John Bradford, being martyred at the stake at Smithfield in 1555, was able to say to John Leaf, the young man being burned with him: 'Be of good comfort, brother; for we shall have a merry supper with the Lord this night.'

Notice the emphasis upon 'this night'. Was not this the very promise which the Lord Jesus Christ himself gave to the dying thief who had repented of his sin and turned to the Saviour? 'And Jesus said to him, "Assuredly, I say to you, today you will be with me in paradise"' (Luke 23:43).

One thing more: the vision of God will be *a never-ending sight*. It will never cease, it will never fail, it will never grow stale in any way. We shall never become so 'used' to it such that, in the well-known phrase, familiarity will breed contempt. The vision will remain fresh and new for ever. Our sight of God will be eternal. On this earth we can get tired even of the loveliest of views, or even of the sight of one another. Where the sight of God is concerned, one moment we have it, the next moment we seem to have lost it, in terms of felt enjoyment. One day we might be on the mountain top, only the next day to be in the dark valley. We experience spiritual seasons when the sun is shining brightly, and then other times when we walk in the darkness and have no light, as Isaiah 50:10 expresses it. We are not strangers to Job's cry, 'Oh, that I knew where I might find him' (Job 23:3). No such thing will ever apply in heaven, however. There, things will be permanent, constant and lasting.

Here is Thomas Brooks again. 'Heaven would not be heaven, were it not always day with the soul; did not the soul live in a constant sight and apprehension of God, all the glory of heaven could not make heaven to a glorified soul.' In another of his sermons he describes the change death brings for the believer in this threefold way: a change of our more dark and obscure enjoyment of God for a more clear and sweet enjoyment of him; a change of our imperfect and incomplete enjoyments of God for a more complete and perfect enjoyment of him; and a change of a more inconstant and transient enjoyment of God for a more constant and permanent enjoyment of him. Of course, the very word 'see' at the heart of Revelation 22:4 carries the sense of clarity, directness and knowledge. Be assured of this: once in heaven, we shall never grow weary of seeing God's face, of beholding God's glory, of delighting in God's presence, of basking in God's love, of exploring God's immensities, or of engaging in God's holy worship and service.

Jonathan Edwards on the vision of heaven

Jonathan Edwards (1703-1758) was the only son in a family of eleven children, and he and his wife, Sarah, were themselves to have eleven children of their own. He is rightly regarded as one of a handful of the truly great theologians of the English-speaking world. 'An intellectual and spiritual giant' is how he has been described.

Both his grandfather (Solomon Stoddard) and his father (Timothy Edwards) were ministers. Jonathan Edwards is best known for his ministry at Northampton, Massachusetts, where he began as assistant to his grandfather, and then became the minister himself. There, in days of drift from the original New England puritanism, he preached faithfully the whole counsel of God, and God honoured his own Word, in what became days of a great awakening. Incredibly, however, he was voted out of that pastorate by his people in 1750, having been with them since 1726. He then became a missionary to the Indians at Stockbridge, and, after that, President of the New Jersey College (later Princeton), though he died only two months after taking up that office.

His extensive published works cover a remarkable array of materials. Of particular help and note are *The Religious Affections*, in which he distinguishes between true and false religion by demonstrating the marks of a genuine work of the Holy Spirit in a person, and his works touching upon revival. A number of passages in his writings bear upon the subject and prospect of the beatific vision. Here are some of them, to assist us in our anticipation of seeing God's face.

The first is this: 'The enjoyment of God is the only happiness with which our souls can be satisfied. To go to heaven, fully to enjoy God, is infinitely better than the most pleasant accommodations here. Fathers and mothers, husbands, wives, or children, or the company of earthly friends, are but shadows; but God is the substance. These are but scattered beams, but God is the sun. These are but streams. But God is the ocean.'

Again: 'To be pure in heart is the sure way to obtain the blessedness of seeing God. This is the divine road to the blissful and glorious presence of God, which, if we take it, will infallibly lead us thither.

'God is the giver of the pure heart, and he gives it for this very end; that it may be prepared for the blessedness of seeing him. Thus we are taught in the Scriptures. The people of God are sanctified, and their hearts are made pure, that they may be prepared for glory, as vessels are prepared by the potter for the use he designs. They are elected from all eternity to eternal life, and have purity of heart given them, on purpose to fit them for that to which they are chosen.'

This is further applied later in the same sermon. 'Hence we learn how great a thing it is to be an upright and sincere Christian; for all such are pure in heart, and stand entitled to the blessedness of seeing the most high God. The time is coming when they shall assuredly see him; they shall see him who is infinitely greater than all the kings of the earth; they shall see him face to face, shall see as much of his glory and beauty as the eyes of their souls are capable of beholding. They shall not only see him for a few moments, or an hour, but they shall dwell in his presence, and shall sit down for ever to drink in the rays of his glory. They shall see him invested in all this majesty, with smiles and love in his countenance; they shall see him, and converse with him, as their nearest and best friend.

'Thus shall they see him soon. The intervening moments fly swiftly, the time is even at the door, when they shall be admitted to this blessedness.'

One of Edwards' choicest works is *Charity and its Fruits*, being his sermons on 1 Corinthians 13. In the closing chapter of this work is this magnificent material upon our subject. It is a fairly lengthy single paragraph, but every word in it counts.

'There, even in heaven, dwells the God from whom every stream of holy love, yea, every drop that is, or ever was, proceeds. There dwells God the Father, God the Son, and God the Spirit, united as one, in infinitely dear, and incomprehensible, and mutual, and eternal love. There dwells God the Father, who is the father of mercies, and so the father of love, who so loved the world as to give his only-begotten Son to die for it. There dwells Christ, the Lamb of God, the prince of peace and love, who so loved the world that he shed his blood, and poured out his soul unto death for men. There dwells the great Mediator, through whom all the divine love is expressed toward men, and by whom the fruits of that love have been purchased, and through whom they are communicated, and through whom love is imparted to the hearts of all God's people. There dwells Christ in both his natures, the human and the divine, sitting on the same throne with the Father. And there dwells the Holy Spirit –

the Spirit of divine love, in whom the very essence of God, as it were, flows out, and is breathed forth in love, and by whose immediate influence all holy love is shed abroad in the hearts of all the saints on earth and in heaven. There, in heaven, this infinite fountain of love – this eternal Three in One – is set open without any obstacle to hinder access to it, as it flows for ever. There this glorious God is manifested, and shines forth, in full glory, in beams of love. And there this glorious fountain for ever flows forth in streams, yea, in rivers of love and delight, and these rivers swell, as it were, to an ocean of love, in which the souls of the ransomed may bathe with the sweetest enjoyment, and their hearts, as it were, be deluged with love!'

6

THE REST OF HEAVEN

The verse of the book of Revelation that we are to consider in this chapter is a famous one, not least because it is often read at the graveside during funeral services. Maybe you have heard the words without necessarily knowing where in the Bible they come from – or even that they are in the Bible at all.

Our subject is the rest of heaven, or the heavenly rest, and it is spoken of in 14:13. 'Then I heard a voice from heaven saying to me, "Write: 'Blessed are the dead who die in the Lord from now on.' " "Yes," says the Spirit, "that they may rest from their labours, and their works follow them."'

This fourteenth chapter of Revelation is a magnificent chapter. It opens (verses 1-5) with a glorious picture of the 'Lamb standing on Mount Zion, and with him one hundred and forty-four thousand having his Father's name' (or better, 'his name and his Father's name') 'written on their foreheads'. That is to say: the Lord Jesus Christ (risen, ascended, glorified and reigning) having his chosen, saved and blood-bought people together with him, secure in him, and gathered by him in heaven.

This is followed (verses 6-13) with John's vision of three 'flying angels' or 'angels in flight', each with a message to proclaim – messages of salvation and judgment, of blessings and woes, of gladness and warning. The first announces that the hour of God's judgment is come; the second that Babylon (a symbol of the world set against God and the gospel) is already fallen; and the third that the worshippers of the beast are to be sent to everlasting torment. There is a choice reference in verse 6 to 'the everlasting gospel' being preached 'to those who dwell on the earth – to every nation, tribe, tongue, and people', and a clarion call in verse 7 to 'Fear God and give glory to him'.

Then the chapter concludes (verses 14-20) with a solemn picture of the end of the world, the final judgment, under the figure of a harvest.

The verse which is taking our particular attention (v.13) comes at the end of the third angel's message, which declares the everlasting punishment of those who, at the end of the day, are not on the Lord's side but are on the devil's side. Yet directly against that dark background comes the precious truth and rich comfort of our verse. In terms of the original circumstances of the book of Revelation, it was intended to bring special support and encouragement to persecuted Christians, and not least to those who would be put to death for the gospel. Yet it is of far wider application than that. There is comfort here for all believers, in all generations and at all times, as well as strong implicit challenge for those who are not.

There are three dimensions to observe concerning the rest of heaven, which we may call a rest 'in', a rest 'from' and a rest 'for'.

Rest 'in'
This rest that is spoken of – 'that they may rest from their labours' – where is it? Where is it to be found? Where can it be enjoyed? The answer is: in heaven. That may seem desperately obvious; but think carefully about it.

For a start, endless multitudes of unbelievers make their rest in this life, on this earth, here and now. It could be, even as you read this, that you are among them. Perhaps you have decided to read this book, and have even persevered with your self-imposed task to this point, because somehow you are curious about heaven, or even imagine that you might be qualified to have some part in it. You are maybe even under the delusion that everybody automatically goes there, though I trust the folly of that view has already been demonstrated. Yet, whatever your thoughts upon the matter, you are still making your rest squarely right now where you are, and have no serious thought of the life to come. Do you argue like this? 'This life is all there is, so of course I'm making the most of it.' Or, if you are not absolutely certain that this life is all there is, do you take the view that 'in case it is, and since probably it is, with no accountablity to anyone and nothing after death, I'll put all my eggs into this world's basket'? For in exactly such a way, many men, women, young people live, and die, and go to hell.

As if that is not serious enough, however, far too many Christians live in pretty much the same way – to all appear- ances, anyway, from how you hear them talk and how you observe them live, though it might shock and offend them to be told so. The result is that you can often barely tell the difference between 'believers' and 'unbelievers', and for this reason: too many 'Christians' are too much at home, too comfortable, too settled in, living for this life, looking to 'make it' (whatever that means) in this life, with very little thought for, meditation on or anticipation of that life to come which the Lord Jesus Christ has purchased for and promised to his own. Paul commands us, 'If then you were raised with Christ, seek those things which are above, where Christ is, sitting at the right hand of God. Set your mind on things above, not on things on the earth. For you died, and your life is hidden with Christ in God' (Col. 3:1-3).

In stark contrast, Abraham and other 'heroes of faith' of whom we read in Hebrews 11 were of a very different stamp. They knew something we need to know – or, at least, something we need to re-learn or be reminded of. Our rest is not here. In a sense, every Christian faces a paradox in this life: that of resting in the Lord, but of experiencing a continual restlessness. This present world is a restless place for the true Christian to live in, because it is not our resting place. Heaven is. Here (to use the language of Hebrews 11) we are like strangers in a foreign country, living in tents. And what is the point and nature of tents? They are temporary. You set them up and you take them down. They are designed for those who are on the move. And Christians are on the move. 'They go from strength to strength; every one of them appears before God in Zion' (Ps. 84:7).

Only heaven is 'the city which has foundations, whose builder and maker is God' (Heb. 11:10). Until then, the church of Christ bears the character of a 'happy band of pilgrims' (or should do so if she is faithful to her true calling and character), desiring 'a better, that is, a heavenly country' (Heb. 11:16). That same verse goes on, most encouragingly, to record: 'Therefore God is not ashamed to be called their God, for he has prepared a city for them.'

Does a traveller settle down to take his permanent rest while he is still 'on the way'? No! He presses on to the journey's end, and then he rests. Only then does he stop travelling and settle down. The Christian's journey's end is heaven – and, more completely, God himself in heaven.

> Our God is the end of the journey,
> His pleasant and glorious domain.   W Vernon Higham

I've found a Friend, O such a Friend!
    All power to Him is given,
To guard me on my onward course,
    And bring me safe to heaven.
The eternal glories gleam afar,
    To nerve my faint endeavour;
So now to watch! to work! to war!
    And then – to rest for ever.   J G Small

'There remains therefore a rest for the people of God' (Heb. 4:9).

Rest 'from'

If you rest, you rest *from*, don't you? You may go home at teatime and rest from the work that has been occupying you through the day. Or if you take a holiday you have a more extended rest from the regular cycle of work or study. So we associate these two words together quite naturally: 'rest from'.

With respect to this rest in heaven, however, what is that a rest from? The angel's message to John speaks of 'labours'. What that contains is beautifully gathered up in the following words. It means, 'resting from ... all the troubles, sorrows, and sufferings, from all the calamities, infirmities, and miseries of this frail mortal state; no sin shall affect them, no sorrow shall afflict them, no danger affright them'.[15] Just think of that!

Part of the glorious inheritance laid up in heaven for every believer is this. There we shall have no more struggles with sin; no more battles with Satan; no more bodily weakness, poorliness or pain; no more sorrow, grief or tears; no more anxieties or cares; no more bad moods, angry words, dark looks, sad misunderstandings or fallings out; no more 'self' rising up to rule the roost and cause trouble; no more divisions and quarrels between Christians that spoil everything, and no more of the various troubles and trials that attend our particular callings; no more dangers, accidents and fears, no more deaths and partings; no more obstacles in the way of the gospel; no more failures, discouragements or disappointments in Christian service or shortfalls in holiness; no more grievings of our gracious God (Father, Son and Holy Spirit).

Moreover, not only will all grievous things be gone, but all good things will be transformed. Prayer will be turned to praise. Faith will have vanished into sight. Preaching Christ will have given way to beholding him and seeing the King in his beauty. Evangelism and missionary outreach will have been completed, with 'all the ransomed church of God ... saved to sin no more'. All of Christ's sheep will be safe in Christ's fold. What a prospect and what a glory!

All of this is true, of course, in essence, immediately upon death, for to die is 'to be absent from the body and to be present with the Lord' (2 Cor. 5:8). It is 'to depart and be with Christ, which is far better' (Phil. 1:23). But, in terms of the whole scenario in Revelation 14, there will be – how can we describe it? – a degree of perfection and completion reserved for that final consummation 'after all the battles are fought, after Babylon is fallen, after the wicked are sent to hell, when the judgment day is past'.[16]

Yet there still remains one further thing to be considered.

Rest 'for'
There is a double-edge to this 'rest for': for whom? and for how long? Both matters are very important, so we shall take them in turn.

First, *rest for whom*? We are not left to decide for
ourselves, for our verse is very plain and explicit. 'Blessed
are the dead who die in the Lord', is what we read. That is
to say, not all the dead, not everyone who dies, but only
some. The words, literally rendered, are 'the ones in the
Lord dying'. They, and only they, are 'blessed'.

And who are they? The Bible describes them in different ways. They are those chosen by God, in Christ, 'before
the foundation of the world' (Eph. 1:4); those who are given
by the Father to the Son and whom the Son, consequently,
has 'by no means cast out' (John 6:37); those whose sins
Christ bore 'in his own body on the tree' (1 Pet. 2:24), and
for whom Christ 'suffered .. the just for the unjust' to bring
them to God (1 Pet. 3:18). They are those who know themselves to be sinful, fallen, corrupt, helpless and far from
God, by their very nature (Ps. 51:5; Eph. 2:3), yet who have
been brought to see in God's dear Son, the Lord Jesus Christ,
the all-sufficient provision for their every need (2 Cor. 8:9).
They have been 'born again' or 'born from above' (John
3:3), redeemed 'with the precious blood of Christ' (1 Pet.
1:19) and brought into the family of God (Eph. 2:19). They
are those who demonstrate that all of this is true by living a
life which adorns the gospel and by persevering to the end
(Titus 2:10; Matt. 24:13). In a word, God has saved them,
and it is all of grace (Eph. 2:8).

It must be emphasized, then, that the only rest is for those
who 'die in the Lord' – those who die, as someone has put
it, in the faith of the Lord, in the fear of the Lord and in the
favour of the Lord. Such, and such only, are 'blessed', which
very word speaks of the favour and kindness and grace of
God. Let Robert Murray M'Cheyne speak on this point. 'It
is not *all* the dead who are blessed. There is no blessing on

the Christless dead; they rush into an *undone* eternity, unpardoned, unholy. You may put their body in a splendid coffin; you may print their name in silver on the lid; you may bring the company of mourners to the funeral, in suits of solemn black; you may lay the coffin slowly in the grave; you may spread the greenest sod above it; you may train the sweetest flowers to grow over it; you may cut a white stone, and grave a gentle epitaph to their memory; still it is but the funeral of a damned soul. You cannot write "*blessed*" where God hath written "*cursed*".'[17]

Then, *rest for how long*? In two words: for ever. The Greek is 'from now' (that is, from now on, from henceforth). This is not a momentary rest or a temporary rest, but an eternal and everlasting rest. Do not look to the grave – look beyond it! Look to being 'absent from the body and present with the Lord'. Look to the immediate reality of heaven itself, to the future glory of the resurrection morning, to the new heavens and new earth where righteousness dwells, to the many mansions of the Father's house. Look 'to Mount Zion and to the city of the living God, the heavenly Jerusalem, to an innumerable company of angels, to the general assembly and church of the first-born who are registered in heaven, to God the judge of all, to the spirits of just men made perfect, to Jesus the mediator of the new covenant, and to the blood of sprinkling that speaks better things than that of Abel' (Heb. 12:22-24).

A word of explanation needs to be added in connection with the words at the end of our verse: 'and their works follow them'. First of all, it is a proper distinction to make in saying that we shall rest from our 'labours' but not from all our 'works'. Heaven is not (and never will be) a place of idleness. For a start, the praise of God in heaven continues

day and night without ceasing. Once there, we shall be like
the angels of God in this respect – while nothing will be
toilsome, laborious or painful about our work, every moment
will be spent in the delightful worship and service of our
glorious and gracious God. What a change, what a difference
this will present from our earthly worship and service. Here
we so easily become weary, we faint, we give up, we find
our strength unequal either to the task itself or our zeal in
it. Not so in heaven! There will be no fatigue, no dullness,
no shortfall there! We are very conscious of our danger of
becoming battle-weary in this life. This hot day of weariness,
though, will not last for ever, for, as one has put it, 'the sun
is nearing the horizon', and will shortly rise again with a
brighter day than any of us have ever seen.

But what of our works 'following' us? What does that
imply? Certainly there is the sense of no labour for the Lord
here upon the earth ever being lost, wasted, or in vain (1
Cor. 15:58). Whatever has been done here truly in his name,
and for his sole glory, will have a continuing fruitfulness to
his praise. There is the aspect of Hebrews 6:10 as well: 'For
God is not unjust to forget your work and labour of love
which you have shown towards his name, in that you have
ministered to the saints, and do minister.' It is not, of course,
on account of our works that we shall be accepted. That can
never be, for salvation is of the Lord, and all of grace. Yet
still, nothing done truly in Christ's name (even the cup of
cold water mentioned in Matthew 25) goes unrewarded or
unregarded.

The point is worth making that our works *follow* us; they
do not go before us, or arrive in heaven before we get there.
That could never be. We have one, and only one, who is our
forerunner – 'even Jesus' (Heb. 6:20), and no one can take

his place. He and his finished work have led the way. Our works neither precede us to heaven nor do they march in with us at our side. They come behind – the best place for them! Yet how wonderfully kind and gracious of our God that he who gives us good works then rewards us for them.

It is death that brings us to this unchangeable, eternal rest, and which explains how a Christian's death-day is better than his birthday, and why a believer's dying day is his best day (Eccl. 7:1). This accounts for the fact that so many of the martyrs welcomed the messengers who came to tell them of their impending execution, hugged the stake, or clapped their hands in the midst of the flames.

Before we move on, it is worth adding this note as well. How the consideration of such a verse as this should help us in practical areas that we all must face: not mourning immoderately at the death of any believer; not being afraid of death itself, but rather longing for it, not primarily in order to be rid of our troubles but in order that we might be taken up in a clearer and fuller enjoyment of God; and stirring ourselves actually to prepare for our dying day, beseeching grace and help so as, when the appointed time comes, to die well. Is this not part of *the* great business of life?

Let an illustration from Ryle gather things up. 'There is a pass in Scotland called Glencoe, which supplies a beautiful illustration of what heaven will be to the man who comes to Christ. The road through Glencoe carries the traveller up a long and steep ascent, with many a little winding and many a little turn in its course. But when the top of the pass is reached, a stone is seen by the wayside, with these simple words engraven on it: "Rest, and be thankful". Those words describe the feelings with which every one who comes to

Christ will at length enter heaven. The summit of the narrow way will be won. We shall cease from our weary journeying, and sit down in the kingdom of God. We shall look back over all the way of life with thankfulness, and see the perfect wisdom of every little winding and turn in the steep ascent by which we were led. We shall forget the toils of the upward journey in the glorious rest. Here in this world our sense of rest in Christ at best is feeble and partial: but, "when that which is perfect is come, then that which is in part shall be done away". Thanks be unto God, a day is coming when believers shall rest perfectly, and be thankful'.[18]

Richard Baxter on the rest of heaven
Richard Baxter (1615-1691) was born at Rowtan, near High Ercal, in Shropshire. His father, a man of some standing, had a small freehold estate at Eaton-Constantine, some five miles southeast of Shrewsbury.

Baxter is perhaps best known for his ministry at Kidderminster, which lasted for over fifteen years. That ministry still stands as a model of the pastoral and preaching office, and was blessed abundantly by God. The town comprised some 800 homes and 2,000 people – 'an ignorant, rude and revelling people' when Baxter arrived among them, though things did not stay that way. In his own words: '... when I came thither first there was about one family in a street that worshipped God and called on his name, and when I came away there were some streets where there was not past one family in the side of a street that did not so, and that did not, by professing serious godliness, give us hope of their sincerity.'

He preached twice on the Lord's Day and once on Thursdays. On Thursday evenings he would answer questions about the sermons in his house. On Monday and Thursday afternoons he and his assistant catechised fourteen families between them. Another's account of these years is as follows: 'Baxter found the place like a piece of dry and barren earth; ignorance and profaneness, like natives of the soil, grew very luxuriant; but by the divine blessing upon both his labour and cultivation, the face of paradise appeared there in all the fruits of righteousness.'

His published writings are many, and include *The Reformed Pastor*, *Call to the Unconverted*, *A Christian Directory* (which contains more than a million words, and is intended to direct Christians 'how to use their knowledge and faith; how to improve all helps and means, and to perform all duties; how to overcome temptations, and to escape or mortify every sin'); and *The Saints' Everlasting Rest*.

It is from this last mentioned volume that the following excerpts are taken with respect to the rest of heaven. The sheer scope and fulness of Baxter's treatment of his subject is remarkable, and impresses upon us how largely these things are neglected in our own day, preaching and Christian experience. The book opens with the quotation of its headline text: 'There remaineth therefore a rest unto the people of God' (Heb. 4:9, AV). It then proceeds in sixteen chapters, covering, for example, the preparatives for and excellencies of the saints' rest; the character of those for whom it is designed and the great misery of those who 'besides losing the saints' rest, lose the enjoyments of time, and suffer the torments of hell'; the necessity of diligently seeking the saints' rest; how to discern our title to it and the duty of the people of God to excite others to seek this rest; the fact that this rest is not to be expected on earth, linked with the importance of leading a heavenly life upon the earth, with directions how to do so; and the nature and importance of heavenly contemplation.

Here is part of the third section of Baxter's work, that dealing with the excellencies of the saints' rest. He treats of nine of these, of which here are two: that it will be seasonable and that it will be suitable. I have taken the liberty of breaking up the one long paragraph on each.

On *how seasonable* the saints' rest will be, Baxter writes this. 'He that expects the fruit of his vineyard at the season, and makes his people "like a tree planted by rivers of water, that bringeth forth his fruit in his season", will also give them the crown in his season. He that will have a word of joy spoken in season to him that is weary, will surely cause the time of joy to appear in the fittest season. They who are not weary in well-doing, shall, if they faint not, reap in due season. If God giveth rain even to his enemies, both the former and the latter in its season, and reserveth the appointed weeks of harvest, and covenants that there shall be day and night in their season, then surely the glorious harvest of the saints shall not miss its season. Doubtless, he who would not stay a day longer than the promise, but brought Israel out of Egypt on the self-same day when the four hundred and thirty years expired, neither will he fail of one day or hour of the fittest season for his people's glory.

'When we have had in this world a long night of darkness, will not the day-breaking and the rising of the Sun of righteousness be then seasonable? When we have passed a long and tedious journey through no small dangers, is not home then seasonable? When we have had a long and perilous war, and received many a wound, would not a peace, with victory, be seasonable?

'Men live in a continual weariness, especially the saints, who are most weary of that which the world cannot feel: some weary of a blind mind, some of a hard heart, some of their daily doubts and fears, some of the want of spiritual joys, and some of the sense of God's wrath. And when a poor Christian hath desired, and prayed, and waited for deliverance many years, is it not then seasonable? We lament that we do not find a Canaan in the wilderness, or the songs of Sion in a strange land – that we have not a harbour in the main ocean, nor our rest in the heat of the day, nor heaven before we leave the earth; and would not all this be very unseasonable?'

On *how suitable* the saints' rest is, this is what Baxter has to say. 'The new nature of the saints doth suit their spirits to this rest. Indeed, their holiness is nothing else but a spark taken from this element, and by the Spirit of Christ kindled in their hearts: the flame whereof, mindful of its own divine original, ever tends to the place from whence it comes. Temporal crowns and kingdoms could not make a rest for saints. As they were not redeemed with so low a price, neither are they endued with so low a nature. As God will have from them a spiritual worship suited to his own spiritual being, he will provide them with a spiritual rest suitable to their spiritual nature.

The knowledge of God and his Christ, a delightful complacency in that mutual love, and everlasting rejoicing in the enjoyment of our God, with a perpetual singing of his high praises; this is heaven for a saint. Then we shall live in our own element. We are now as the fish in a vessel of water, only so much as will keep them alive; but what is that to the ocean? We have a little air let in to us, to afford us breathing; but what is that to the sweet and fresh gales upon mount Sion? We have a beam of the sun to lighten our darkness, and a warm ray to keep us from freezing; but then we shall live in its light, and be revived by its heat for ever.

As are the natures of the saints, such are their desires; and it is the desires of our renewed nature to which this rest is suited. While our desires remain corrupted and misguided, it is a far greater mercy to deny them, yea, to destroy them, than to satisfy them; but those which are spiritual are of his own planting, and he will surely water them, and give the increase. He quickened our hunger and thirst for righteousness, that he might make us happy in a full satisfaction.

Christian, this is a rest after thine own heart; it contains all that thy heart can wish; that which thou longest, prayest, labourest for, there thou shalt find it all. Thou hadst rather have God in Christ than all the world; there thou shalt have him. What wouldst thou not give for assurance of his love? There thou shalt have assurance without suspicion. Desire what thou canst, and ask what thou wilt, as a Christian, and it shall be given thee, not only to half the kingdom, but to the enjoyment both of kingdom and King. This is a life of desire and prayer, but that is a life of satisfaction and enjoyment. This rest is very suitable to the saints' necessities also, as well as to their natures and desires. It contains whatsoever they truly wanted; not supplying them with gross, created comforts, which, like Saul's armour on David, are more burden than benefit. It was Christ and perfect holiness which they most needed, and with these shall they be supplied.'

7

THE PROMISES OF HEAVEN

In a very special sense, the Bible is God's book of promises. It is much more than this, but it is certainly a treasure-store of his divine promises. As we continue our study of the doctrine of heaven in this last book of the Bible, it is God's promises which come now to the fore.

Let us begin with a reminder. When the book of Revelation was first written, it was directed to seven churches in Asia Minor. The Lord Jesus Christ addressed a letter to each of these churches, and these letters are recorded for us in chapters 2 and 3 of the book – probably a couple of the most familiar chapters in the whole of the book, and as far as many ever get in their study of this part of Scripture. In my commentary on Revelation, there is a short section setting out some basic ground rules for interpreting these letters to the churches, one of which is the insistence that, as well as being actual churches at the time (at Ephesus, Smyrna, Pergamos, Thyatira, Sardis, Philadelphia, and Laodicea), these churches are also representative of the varying states and conditions of the church of the Lord Jesus Christ at all times, in all its ups and downs, its healths and poorlinesses, its prosperings and declensions. This representativeness may be set out as follows:

Ephesus: the church that had lost its first love for Christ
Smyrna: the church suffering persecution for the gospel
Pergamos: the church riddled with compromise
Thyatira: the over-tolerant church

Sardis: the church which prided itself on its reputation for being so alive, yet in reality was well on the way to being dead

Philadelphia: the church full of opportunity and prospects

Laodicea: the lukewarm church, neither hot nor cold.

In each of these seven letters to the churches, the Lord Jesus Christ adopts a plan along the lines of exposing the problem, writing a prescription and then adding a promise. It is with these magnificent divine promises that we are presently concerned. Each one comes with the exhortation, 'He who has an ear, let him hear what the Spirit says to the churches'. Each one is addressed to 'him who overcomes' (that is to say, to true believers who demonstrate that they are true believers by enduring to the end and gaining the victory at last; those who keep faith, hope, love and obedience to Christ, through all the thick and thin of trials, afflictions and pressures to compromise the truth or deny the Saviour). And in each one the Lord Jesus Christ is himself the 'Yes' and 'Amen' of the promises (2 Cor. 1:20); 'I will give', he says, or 'I will make', 'I will write' or 'I will grant'.

The plan adopted now may seem a trifle ambitious, since each of these promises is worthy of close and detailed exposition on its own. Indeed several complete books have been written on Revelation 2 and 3. Here, however, I wish to give a broad view of all seven promises, in order that we might be thrilled with a sense of the whole – these promises of heaven that are from Christ, through Christ and in Christ, for every true believer. It ought to take our breath away!

1 Delighting in Christ

The first of the promises is found in 2:7. 'To him who overcomes I will give to eat from the tree of life, which is in the midst of the paradise of God.' Reading these words, our minds should go straight back to the Garden of Eden where Adam and Eve walked with God in a perfect sweetness and intimacy of fellowship and blessed delight. In the midst of the garden was the tree of life. All that blessedness was lost, however, when they sinned against God and came under his curse. As a result, 'sin entered the world, and death through sin, and thus death spread to all men, because all sinned' (Rom. 5:12), and so there we are (all of us, by nature): sinners under the judgment of God.

Yet what has happened in the gospel? Nothing less than this: paradise lost has become paradise regained. Indeed, more than that: on account of the Lord Jesus Christ's death on the cross, paradise regained (heaven itself) is far greater and far more glorious even than paradise before it was lost. So once again we may recall these lines:

> Where He displays His healing power,
> Death and the curse are known no more;
> In Him the tribes of Adam boast
> More blessings than their father lost.
>
> Isaac Watts

What the sin of Adam lost, the grace of Christ restores. Christ himself declares: 'I have come that they may have life, and that they may have it more abundantly' (John 10:10). There are all the gospel blessings of sins forgiven, curse removed, fellowship with God restored, heaven opened. All such things are symbolised under this figure in 2:7 of eating 'from the tree of life, which is in the midst of the paradise of

God'. 'Paradise' is a word of Persian origin meaning 'pleasure park', where there would be meadows, gardens and the splendour of a royal residence. The Greek version of the Old Testament applied it to the Garden of Eden. Jesus' promise here is a picture of the loveliness, delight and intimacy which believers will have with him in glory. This is the full life of God in the soul. Heaven is a royal residence indeed! 'In your presence is fullness of joy; at your right hand are pleasures for evermore' (Ps. 16:11).

The apostle Paul works out the Adam-Christ theme exquisitely in Romans 5, of course. Observe the several contrasts there. There is 'the one man's offence' as a result of which 'many died', and 'the grace of God and the gift by the grace of the one man, Jesus Christ' which 'abounded to many' (v.15). There is 'the judgment which came from one offence' and 'resulted in condemnation', and 'the free gift which came from many offences' and 'resulted in justification' (v.16). And so it continues, verse by verse, climaxing in verse 19: 'For as by one man's disobedience many were made sinners, so also by one man's obedience many will be made righteous'; and in verses 20-21: 'But where sin abounded, grace abounded much more, so that as sin reigned in death, even so grace might reign through righteousness to eternal life through Jesus Christ our Lord.'

2 Victorious through Christ

The second of the promises is found in 2:10-11. 'Be faithful unto death, and I will give you the crown of life.... He who overcomes shall not be hurt by the second death.' It is, in fact, a double promise: the promise of being given 'the crown of life', and the promise of not being hurt by 'the second death'.

What is meant by 'the crown of life'? It is the victor's place of honour in God's new creation. The victory over sin, death, Satan and hell has been won for us by the Lord Jesus Christ. It is his victory, and he gives to his people the spoils of victory to share. This 'crown' is mentioned on a number of occasions in Scripture. Paul calls it both 'an imperishable crown' (1 Cor. 9:25) and 'the crown of right-eousness' (2 Tim. 4:8). James calls it 'the crown of life' (Jas. 1:12). Peter calls it 'the crown of glory that does not fade away' (1 Pet. 5:4). What an encouragement this is that the Lord Jesus gives us, and what a prize of grace that he holds out for us.

What about 'the second death'? That striking phrase signifies final and absolute separation for ever from the God who is 'the fountain of life' (Ps. 36:9), as well as the fount of all love, joy, grace and salvation. It refers to 'the lake of fire' (Rev. 20:15), the destiny of the wicked (21:8). It is the eternal ruin and everlasting punishment of both body and soul, which will be consummated at the last judgment, when 'those who have done evil' will 'come forth ... to the resurrection of condemnation' (John 5:29). Yet none of this separation and torment and punishment can touch or hurt the Christian any longer. Why not? For one reason, and one reason only: 'There is therefore now no condemnation to those who are in Christ Jesus, who do not walk according to the flesh, but according to the Spirit' (Rom. 8:1).

It follows, of course, that these are the only two possible alternatives: 'the crown of life' or 'the second death'. Pos-sessing the former, means deliverance from the latter, even though (and the persecuted believers at Smyrna knew about this at first hand) holding firmly to the faith and refusing to deny the Lord Jesus Christ could cost you your life.

'When he (ie, the Christian) approaches the end of the conflict, death itself, whether it comes amidst all the endearments of a Christian home, or in the tortures of a cruel martrydom, is compelled to be no longer the messenger of a curse, but the servant of a king, bearing the crown of life, and placing it on the conqueror's brow, and confessing that he (ie, death) is for ever vanquished ... And at the last, amidst the crash of dissolving nature, and the fires that purify an accursed world, and consume all the works and monuments of a sinful race, he (ie, the believer) shall stand in his glorified and immortal body calm and secure beneath the spreading wings of eternal love.'[19]

3 Made like Christ

The third of the promises is found in 2:17. 'To him who overcomes I will give some of the hidden manna to eat. And I will give him a white stone, and on the stone a new name written which no one knows except him who receives it.' There is a lot there to take in: 'the hidden manna', 'a white stone', and 'on the stone a new name written'. What a full verse and what a rich promise this contains from the Lord Jesus Christ, and what mystery too. What does it all add up to?

Consider first of all 'the hidden manna'. This recalls God's provision for his people throughout the days of the wilderness wanderings, when he sent them manna from heaven to eat. A pot of this manna was kept inside the ark of the covenant before God as a memorial from one generation to another; it was hidden from view. Here, in particular, it recalls Jesus' teaching in John 6:27: 'Do not labour for the food which perishes, but for the food which endures to everlasting life, which the Son of Man will give you, because God the Father has set his seal on him.' It speaks of the believer's entire satisfaction and nourishment being found in the Lord Jesus Christ alone, which is hidden from all who do not have eyes to see. It recalls the truths that in Christ 'are hidden all the treasures of wisdom and knowledge' (Col. 2:3), and that our life, as believers, 'is hidden with Christ in God' (Col. 3:3). That last statement is immediately followed with this one: 'When Christ who is our life appears, then you also will appear with him in glory' (Col. 3:4).

So far, so good. But what of the reference to 'a white stone' with 'a new name written on it' which only the one receiving it knows. That does not seem so obvious! What is signified, in fact, is something altogether glorious. This is a magnificent picture of what Paul, in 1 Corinthians 1:30, calls 'Christ Jesus, who became for us wisdom from God – and righteousness and sanctification and redemption.' The words of the verse we are looking at speak of the Christian being found in Christ and made like Christ.

The illustration of the white stone comes from one or other (or both) of two ancient customs. The first is the little stones of friendship, called 'tesserae'. Such stones featured a combination of letters on them exclusive to one particular house. They were issued to various friends who had a standing invitation and welcome to the hospitality of that home at any time. However, when a citizen of Pergamos became a Christian (this promise arises at the end of Christ's letter to Pergamos) these stones, and the privileges that went with them, were often withdrawn. It was part of the cost of being identified with the Lord Jesus Christ. In contrast (and this is the point) nothing that the Lord Jesus Christ has done for us or promised us in the gospel (including that 'holiness, without which no one will see the Lord', as Hebrews 12:14 describes it) will ever be withdrawn from the true believer. 'For the gifts and the calling of God are irrevocable' (Rom. 11:29).

The second possible background concerning the white stone is from the court of law. In court cases, a white stone represented acquittal and pardon, whereas a black stone spelled guilt and condemnation. On the white stones were written the names of the innocent, and on the black stones the names of the guilty. Regularly in Revelation, white is the colour of purity, holiness and victory. In and through the Lord Jesus Christ the believer has been given the white stone and the promise of all the grace that we shall ever need – not only in respect of salvation from sin's guilt and penalty, but deliverance as well from sin's very presence and power: full salvation and ultimate complete sanctification! Nothing less than that! The 'new name' written on it (again there is this sense of hiddenness, since this new name 'no one knows except him who receives it') expresses the individual inner character of each believer. Jesus 'calls his own sheep by name and leads them out' (John 10:3). It is also a strong reminder that every true Christian has been 'born again' (John 3:3), and being 'in Christ ... is a new creation; old things have passed away; behold, all things have become new' (2 Cor. 5:17).

4 Reigning with Christ

The fourth of the promises extends through 2:26-29. It is made to 'he who overcomes, and keeps my works until the end'. To all such, the Lord Jesus Christ, the Head of the church, promises 'to him I will give power over the nations ... and I will give him the morning star'.

What a promise this is! Quoting from Psalm 2, a psalm which begins with a vivid picture of the nations raging and the people plotting 'against the Lord and against his anointed', and which then proceeds to picture, equally vividly, the one who sits in the heavens laughing and holding them in derision and records the promise of the Father giving authority to the Son to rule, judge and possess the nations – just see what is in prospect here: the believer sharing Christ's rule, Christ's authority and Christ's glory with him. Once again, the rule, the authority and the glory are Christ's. They belong to him. However, by virtue of union with him it belongs even to the humblest and most despised believer. His glory becomes our glory, and in his rule, we rule. 'Do you not know that the saints will judge the world?' (1 Cor. 6:2). 'Then the kingdom and dominion, and the greatness of the kingdoms under the whole heaven, shall be given to the people, the saints of the Most High' (Dan. 7:27).

If you were to enquire: how shall we share this?, the answer is by consenting to, approving and applauding all of Christ's judgments which he will denounce against and execute upon the nations. We shall be associated with him and identified with him in his judgments, and shall share with him in his glory. Furthermore, there is an important sense in which this sharing in Christ's rule and reign has already begun and is part of our 'here and now', as the gospel is preached, the cause of God and truth prospers, the kingdom of Christ is established in the building of his church and his enemies are put to flight. Even now God, in his rich mercy and great love towards us, has 'raised us up together, and made us sit together in the heavenly places in Christ Jesus' (Eph. 2:6). We 'reign in life through the one, Jesus Christ' (Rom. 5:17).

All of this is capped most amazingly with verse 28: 'and I will give him the morning star'. The Old Testament background to this is found in Numbers 24:17, where it is prophesied that 'a star shall come out of Jacob; a sceptre shall rise out of Israel'. Note the connection between the 'star' (royal brightness and glory) and the 'sceptre' (kingly rule and authority) in relation to our present passage in Revelation. The morning star is Christ himself. This is made clear in 22:16, where he says very plainly of himself, 'I am ... the bright and morning star.' It is Christ himself in his splendour and majesty and brightness. It is Christ giving himself to us.

There is something altogether remarkable here: not only do we share in Christ's activities, but we actually possess Christ himself. You will appreciate that this latter is a huge step on from the former, even though the former is mind-blowing enough. The promise is to those who are faithful, those who 'hold fast what you have' (v.25), those who are pure from the defilement of false teaching. As a result of this promise, that prophecy of Daniel 12:3 will be fulfilled: 'Those who are wise shall shine like the brightness of the firmament.' So will the words of Jesus himself: 'Then the righteous will shine forth as the sun in the kingdom of their Father. He who has ears to hear, let him hear!' (Matt. 13:43). Had you thought of that?

5 Acknowledged by Christ

The fifth of the promises is found in 3:4-5. Here the Lord Jesus Christ records to the church: 'You have a few names even in Sardis who have not defiled their garments; and they shall walk with me in white, for they are worthy.' The phrase 'a few names even in Sardis' stands out, both the 'few' and the 'even'. Their Lord and Saviour observes them, for he knows precisely who are his, not least in the professing church. The true spiritual state of each one of us never escapes his attention. He is never 'taken in'. He knows what is in a man (John 2:25). Consequently, is it not blessed indeed to be pronounced 'worthy' by God? It can only be as we are reckoned so by his grace, for all God's dealings with us are of grace, and grace alone, from first to last.

One of the most wonderful and amazing things, as we contemplate the future glory that is yet to be revealed, is surely this: the Lord Jesus Christ acknowledging us before his Father and his angels – and doing so not grudgingly or reservedly, but with delight, with pleasure and with joy. Us? Can it really mean us – the likes of you and me, who have grieved him and sinned so much against him, and who still give him such cause for sadness? Yes indeed! And the assurance of this divine acknowledgment is at the heart of this promise. Observe verse 5: 'He who overcomes shall be clothed in white garments, and I will not blot out his name from the book of life; but I will confess his name before my Father and before his angels.'

The emphatic negative cast of Jesus' promise 'I will not blot out his name from the book of life', is a way of asserting the strongest possible positive: all the names thus written by God in the book of life are safely inscribed there and are not subject to erasure. 'Thus the perseverance of the saints to glory confirms their foreordination in the heavenly register of the redeemed.'[20]

Yet there is still more, and what a promise this is: 'I will confess his name.' As if to say, 'this one's mine! I died for this one! this one is clothed in my righteousness! this one is a sheep of my flock! this one's my friend!' Can you imagine it? We are used to folk in this life turning against us and refusing to acknowledge us. So what a day it will be when the Lord Jesus Christ, our blessed and beloved Saviour, confesses us before his Father and his angels! And, of course, there is a linkage here with what has just been mentioned above, for it is those names written in the book of life who will be confessed by the Lord Jesus Christ.

This whole fifth promise, says one, 'brings us ... to the great central idea of the blessedness and glory of the spiritual kingdom. It assures the victor of perfect personal holiness, entire conformity to the divine image, and of a public recognition of his divine relationship'.[21]

May these words be true of us:

> I'm not ashamed to own my Lord,
> Or to defend His cause;
> Maintain the honour of His Word,
> The glory of His cross.

And may the same be so with these:

> Then will He own my worthless name
> Before His Father's face;
> And, in the new Jerusalem,
> Appoint my soul a place.
>
> Isaac Watts

6 Secure in Christ

The sixth promise is expressed in 3:11-12, where the key picture is that of the pillar. 'He who overcomes, I will make him a pillar in the temple of my God, and he shall go out no more.' This is especially significant as it arises in the course of the letter to the church at Philadelphia. That whole region was subject to earthquakes which caused strong pillars to topple and magnificent buildings to collapse to the ground in a heap. But, assures the Lord Jesus, there will be no toppling or collapsing for the Christian.

Do you remember the apostle Paul's testimony in 2 Timothy 1:12? 'For this reason I also suffer these things; nevertheless I am not ashamed, for I know whom I have believed and am persuaded that he is able to keep what I have committed to him until that day.' Well, here is why he could give that testimony in such an assured way. The Lord's people are not collapsing pillars but abiding pillars. We are saved not for a moment, but for ever. There is nothing 'here today, gone tomorrow', about the true Christian, the one who is enabled to persevere to the end.

Moreover, this security in Christ for the believer is underscored further as the promise continues: 'And I will write on him the name of my God and the name of the city of my God, the new Jerusalem, which comes down out of heaven from my God. And I will write on him my new name.' A person is known by his or her name. So the language that the Lord Jesus uses here indicates the Christian's true identity: belonging to God, and the Christian's true citizenship: belonging to heaven.

Notice just a little more closely the threefold name written upon the believer. Firstly, says Jesus, there is 'the name of my God', which speaks of divine election (choice), ownership and protection, and recalls the lovely words of blessing upon God's people which are recorded in Numbers 6:24-26 (the Lord blessing and keeping them, making his face shine upon them and being gracious to them, lifting up his countenance upon them and giving them peace), immediately after which God adds 'So they will put my name on the children of Israel, and I will bless them' (v. 27). How striking it is, as well, to observe the Son speaking

of the Father as 'my God', as he did at Calvary (Matt. 27:46).
Secondly, says Jesus, there is 'the name of the city of my
God'. At this very moment 'our citizenship is in heaven,
from which we also eagerly wait for the Saviour, the Lord
Jesus Christ' (Phil. 3:20). The particular reference here in
Revelation, though, strains forward to the complete
assembly of all the saints in heaven, once all have been
gathered in. And, thirdly, says Jesus, there is 'my new name'
– his own new name, that 'name which is above every name'
(Phil. 2:9), given to him by God at his exaltation to heaven
following his finished work upon the earth: the name of the
one who is 'King of kings and Lord of lords' (Rev. 19:16).
Resting upon that finished work, we shall not merely behold
but shall share his glory.

Alongside the highly personal nature of all this for each
Christian individually (the repeated 'he' and 'him' of v.12),
what a special blessedness there will be, then, when all the
people of God are finally gathered together in glory, and
are partaking to the fullest extent of the promises assured
here. What eternal monuments to the praise of God's matchless grace and love and power we shall be!

7 Glorified with Christ

The seventh promise is found in 3:21, and what a promise it
is to complete the sequence. 'To him who overcomes I will
grant to sit with me on my throne, as I also overcame and sat
down with my Father on his throne.' Our union with Christ
is at the heart of things once again. We have everything in
Christ, and nothing apart from Christ. His enthronement is
his people's enthronement – the enthronement of those for
whom he shed his blood and died.

For me, Lord Jesus, thou hast died,
And I have died in thee:
Thou'rt risen, my bands are all untied,
And now thou livest in me;
When purified, made white, and tried,
Thy glory then for me.

Anne Ross Cousin

In Christ, our own glorification is even now a reality. Just recall the golden chain in Romans 8:30, where it is so certain and so assured that it is expressed in the past tense. 'Moreover whom he predestined, these he also called; whom he called, these he also justified; and whom he justified, these he also glorified.'

This very matter is stated and pictured for us by the Saviour in the words of this promise in Revelation. For notwithstanding the present reality of our enthronement and glorification with Christ, there is, quite clearly, a vital future dimension to it as well. Where are we now? Upon the earth. What are we doing now? Travelling through the wilderness. What is true of us now? 'They go from strength to strength; every one of them appears before God in Zion' (Ps. 84:7). What is our testimony now? 'Not that I have already attained, or am already perfected; but I press on, that I may lay hold of that for which Christ Jesus has also laid hold of me ... I press towards the goal for the prize of the upward call of God in Christ Jesus' (Phil. 3:12, 14).

There is a famous remark of the Puritan, John Preston: 'when I die, I shall change my place but not my company.' Exactly so! Right now (3:20) the Lord Jesus sits at our table here on earth, as we enjoy communion and fellowship with him; while in heaven for ever (3:21) we shall sit with Christ upon his and his Father's throne. (Just notice, in passing, that one throne, not two, is spoken of, for Christ is God, the second person of the Godhead). 'He restores our human nature to that height of glory and perfection where the perfect communion of the covenant is again possible and is realised in the highest possible sense of the word.'[22] What a contrast that presents with how we are presently regarded in and by the world. No glory is seen in us. Much of the time little notice is taken of us. Certainly many would rather do without us. But what surprises there will be all round!

Even after so brief and rapid a survey as this, putting all of these promises together you could call them the magnificent seven! Here they are again: delighting in Christ, victorious through Christ, made like Christ, reigning with Christ, acknowledged by Christ, secure in Christ, glorified with Christ. Such is the portion of all those whose names are written in the book of life. Does it include you?

Robert Murray M'Cheyne on the promises of heaven
Robert Murray M'Cheyne (1813-1843) is widely regarded, to God's praise, as one of the choicest Christians who has ever lived. It has been testified of him that 'love to Christ was the great secret of all his devotion and consistency'.

Andrew Bonar, perhaps the closest of all M'Cheyne's friends, has given us this cameo of the man: 'His eminently holy walk and conversation, combined with the deep solemnity of his preaching, was specially felt. The people loved to speak of him. In one place, where a meeting had been intimated, the people assembled, resolved to cast stones at him as soon as he should begin to speak; but no sooner had they begun, than his manner, his look, his words, riveted them all, and they listened with intense eagerness; and before he left the place, the people gathered round him, entreating him to stay and preach to them. One man, who had cast mud at him, was afterwards moved to tears on hearing of his death.'

Born in Edinburgh, the youngest child in a family of five, he was converted to Christ from a worldly life of card playing, dancing and entertainment. M'Cheyne is best remembered for his historic ministry at St Peter's, Dundee. He spoke of God setting him 'down among the noisy merchants and political weavers of this godless town'. Yet heaven-sent revival came in the course of his brief ministry there, and folk stood in the aisles and sat on the pulpit steps, many of them weeping, in order to press into the church to hear him. M'Cheyne was noted for his zeal to promote missionary outreach to the Jewish people, and it was while he, Bonar and others were away on a Mission of Inquiry to Palestine that blessing began to abound in Dundee (William Chalmers Burns was preaching for M'Cheyne at that time). Never strong in bodily health, he died in 1843, a little short of his thirtieth birthday.

The *Memoir and Remains* of M'Cheyne (written and prepared by Bonar) is one of the all-time classics of spiritual literature, and continues to be treasured. Several volumes of his sermons are also available. The two following extracts come from a small book of his sermons on Christ's letters to *The Seven Churches of Asia* in the book of Revelation. I have divided the material into shorter paragraphs.

Here he is, first of all, upon 'the crown of life' and 'the second death' (2:10-11), which he calls 'another of Christ's encouragements'. 'The second death! and are there two deaths? Yes. Have you ever been at a death-bed? Have you ever seen the eyes roll back, the lips quiver, and the hands grow cold and motionless? Have you ever seen the death-bed of an awakened sinner, of one who cried out, Oh for another day! Oh for another hour! Oh for another moment! – of one who was *obliged* to die? Well, then, that is but a shadow of the second death.

When you are walking on the road, and when the sun causes you to see your figure, that is only the shadow – the substance is the real thing; so it is agreed by the soundest divines (and I believe it is true) that God intended the first death to be a type, or shadow, of the second death of the Christless soul; and if the first, the shadow, be so dreadful, what will the second death be? – when it shall be eternally dying, but never dead; when you shall be wishing to die, but are not able!

When you see one ill with fever, he is anxious to get water, but he cannot swallow it; and this is but a type of the burning thirst of those who have died without Christ, when they shall ask for a drop of water to cool their parched tongue.

But it is very different with the believer; death is no death to him, for Christ hath taken away its sting; it is to him an entrance into life; and then he shall not be hurt of the second death – it shall pass by, but shall not touch him. And again, Jesus says, 'Be thou faithful unto death, and I will give thee a crown of life.' It is called in one place a crown of gold, in another a crown of righteousness, in another a crown of glory, and here it is said to be a crown of life – it shall never fade! But what is meant by being faithful unto death? It is to be believing unto the end, to believe unto your dying hour; and then, when God wipes away the tears, Christ shall put on the crown.'

And here he is on the promise of 3:12, which he calls 'the reward Christ offers'. 'There are some of you that would be glad to be stones in the temple; but Christ says of some, that He will make them a *pillar*: there are some of you who would be glad if you just *got in*; but Christ says, you *shall no more go out*. 'And I will write upon him the name of my God.' Even here, one says, I am the Lord's; and another calls himself by the name of Jacob; and another subscribes with his hand unto the Lord, and surnames himself by the name of Israel. But then how *surely it shall be done*, when Christ shall write upon us the name of His God!

Here we are possessed with the world – with money – possessed with those we love too much, with our friends; but we belong to that city, that city which hath foundations, whose builder and maker is God. It shall be said of us, we are born here: and observe, we shall be nearer to God than we are to the saints; for it is written, that we 'are no more strangers and foreigners, but fellow-citizens with the saints, and of the household of God'; we shall be in the same *city* with the saints, but in the same *house* with God, of the household of God.

Is there any other name Christ could write upon us? Is there anything else in heaven or in the earth He could give us? Yes, 'I will write upon him my new name.' Ah! if the Saviour's name were not written upon us, the name of His God would not be written upon us. We must have Christ's name written upon us here; He must write it upon us with His own hand; and then we shall have God's name written upon us there. Let us have Christ's old name here, which is Emmanuel, the seed of the woman; and then He will write upon us His new name, which is 'KING OF KINGS AND LORD OF LORDS'. We shall share in His *kingdom*, we shall share in His *crown*, we shall share in His *glory*.'

8

THE PREPARATION FOR HEAVEN

How do you view 'this life'? Do you see it as something in itself, on its own – in other words, this is it, this life is all there is? Or do you see it as something fundamentally miserable and hard, to be trudged through as best you can, hoping it will not go on too long? Or do you regard it as the gift of God, and so a season to be relished in coming to know God and growing in the knowledge of God, in readiness for being with him in heaven for ever?

The true Christian sees this life very much as a school or training ground, where those who belong to the Lord Jesus Christ are continually being prepared for their lasting home; a time (whether short, medium or long) which all the way through is geared, we might say, to getting ready for and being prepared for heaven. In other words, they view this life from the perspective of eternity. Do you?

If you are not a Christian, you will not. You will be taken up with this life, whether enthusiastically or depressively, elated maybe by some of its experiences, and cast down by others. However, if you are a Christian, if you are one who names the name of Christ and confesses him as your only Saviour, your true delight, the best Beloved of your soul – you to whom Christ is precious: how do you view this life? Actually? Seriously? Consciously?

It is this great matter of this life as a preparation for heaven which is before us in the present chapter – or, at least, one particularly important aspect of it which we glean from the Lord Jesus Christ's own words in Revelation 3:19. 'As many as I love, I rebuke and chasten.' In the previous chapter we were considering the gracious and glorious promises to believers to be found at the end of each of the letters to the seven churches. The verse which takes our attention now arises in the course of the Lord Jesus' letter to the church at Laodicea. This was the lukewarm church, of which he says in verse 15, 'I know your works, that you are neither cold nor hot. I could wish you were cold or hot.'

Central to what Jesus says in 3:19 is his work of rebuking and chastening (or disciplining) his church. This divine work is a vital ingredient in his preparing of each of his people for heaven. What is in view is not punishment but rather: the Lord correcting our faults; the Lord training us up in the way he would have us go and keeping us from wandering off or breaking out into paths and schemes of our own foolish choosing; the Lord developing us, sanctifying us, bringing us towards spiritual maturity; the Lord forming himself in us, so that 'when he is revealed, we shall be like him, for we shall see him as he is' (1 John 3:2).

There are four questions for us to ask concerning this preparation for heaven.

1 In what spirit does Christ do this?

That is to say, what is the manner in which he goes about it? What attitude does he adopt? He tells us clearly in his own words: 'As many as *I love*, I rebuke and chasten.' He does this work in love. His rebukes, his chastenings, his disciplines (to which we might add his tryings and his afflictings) are all tokens of his love. They are not to do us harm but to do us good. They are not negative but positive. They are not the marks of his rejection but the evidence of his adoption. They are not the smitings of his wrath but the favours of his love. They are not his cursings but his blessings. It is all done because he loves us, because we matter to him, because we are important to him and precious to him, and because he would have us thoroughly for himself. He says so.

Look at the emphatic 'I': '*I* love, *I* rebuke and chasten.' We have his word upon it – the word of him who cannot lie and does not change his mind. Will you take him at his word, dear Christian? In fact, he says it three times – once in Proverbs 3:12, once in Hebrews 12:6, and here in Revelation 3:19. How many times does he have to say it before you will believe him? Once alone should be enough, but see how he repeats himself for you!

Do you sometimes ask: what's going on? what's happening to me? what is the Lord doing with me? Do you become mystified? Worse still, do you start fretting or murmuring? Do you ever doubt his love or question his wisdom? Don't! Does he ever appear to you (as we say) cruel to be kind? It is because he loves you so much. He would not bother with you or take such trouble otherwise. He is not willing to leave us to ourselves. He is not content (dare I say it?) to save us and then to leave us to it. 'Though he causes grief, yet he will show compassion according to the multitude of his mercies. For he does not afflict willingly, nor grieve the children of men' (Lam. 3:32f).

It is very revealing to discover how all of this is laid out in Hebrews 12 in terms of God's *adopting* love. Refresh your mind concerning the content of Hebrews 12:3-11. The writer quotes from Proverbs 3: 'My son, do not despise the chastening of the LORD, nor be discouraged when you are rebuked by him; for whom the LORD loves he chastens, and scourges every son whom he receives', and then proceeds to open up that teaching. The fact is that, 'If you endure chastening, God deals with you as with sons; for what son is there whom a father does not chasten?' In other words, our being chastened by God is a proof of him having adopted us as his children, an evidence of our sonship, and not a denial of the same. Whereas, 'if you are without chastening, of which all have become partakers, then you are illegitimate and not sons.' If our human fathers corrected us (because of their love for us), and we respected them for it, then 'shall we not much more readily be in subjection to the Father of spirits and live?'

2 For what end does he do this?

I say 'end', singular, rather than 'ends', plural. In due course I shall mention some subsidiary (though by no means unimportant) 'ends', but for the moment there is just one 'end' to keep in view. What grand, supreme, ultimate end does Christ have in view in all his rebukes, chastenings and disciplines? The answer is this: our holiness in heaven, our fellowship with him there. Always, the Lord's greatest concern for us is our holiness rather than our happiness, for the profoundly simple reason that it is only as we are holy that we shall be happy (although we in our folly so often still do not see that – we would save ourselves a lot of heartache, not to mention a lot of grieving of God, if only we did). This, then, is the great end to which the Lord's love is determined to bring us, and he employs and will employ a whole variety of different means to ensure that end.

This is pure Hebrews 12 again: 'that we may be partakers of his holiness' (12:10). You ask: when and where will this be? The answer comes back: in heaven. God would work this work with heaven in view, so that in eternity and for eternity it might yield the profit. 'Now no chastening seems to be joyful for the present, but grievous; nevertheless, afterwards it yields the peaceable fruit of righteousness to those who have been trained by it' (Heb. 12:11).

It really is true that 'the work which his goodness began, the arm of his strength will complete', to quote Toplady's familiar words. He will not give up. He will not abandon all part way through. He will never lay aside or leave off his work. He is not like us! God's plan is this: he has chosen a people for himself (remember Revelation 7:9), that they (we!) should spend eternity with him in glory. To that end, he labours continually, not least with his rebukes, chastenings and disciplines. And when I say 'he', do not be confused by an apparent interchanging of the first and second persons of the Godhead in the above paragraphs. This work of our preparation for heaven is a classic and choice instance, if ever there was one, of the Saviour's assertion, 'I and my Father are one' (John 10:30).

The context of our present verse in Revelation 3 is very instructive. Immediately after saying, 'As many as I love, I rebuke and chasten' with its following call, 'therefore be zealous and repent', the Lord Jesus Christ speaks of our fellowship with him *here and now* (while still upon the earth) growing ever deeper, richer and purer (v. 20), and our fellowship with him *there and then* (once with him in heaven) when all will be fully realised and consummated (v. 21).

> O for a closer walk with God,
> A calm and heavenly frame,
> A light to shine upon the road
> That leads me to the Lamb!
>
> William Cowper

We misunderstand greatly the Lord's dealings with us day by day to the extent to which we fail to see his ultimate end in all that he has done, is doing, and yet has in mind to do. If you are his child, he will have you for heaven, whatever it takes, and he will prepare you for that throughout your life. A W Pink has a choice remark: 'One breath of paradise will extinguish all the adverse winds of earth. One day in the Father's house will more than balance the years we have spent in this dreary wilderness.'[23] Our great need, therefore, is for the Lord to grant to us the faith and the enabling to lay hold of the future in eager anticipation, and to live somewhat in the present enjoyment of it. It needs to be said of us, as it was said of the Puritan minister Richard Sibbes, 'heaven was in him, before he was in heaven'. Keep right on to the end of the road. Keep right on to the end!

3 Through what means does he do this?

As the verse we are focusing on in this chapter arises from Revelation 3 and this letter of the Lord Jesus Christ to the church at Laodicea, we might answer the question by saying, he does it with his 'knockings'. In verse 20 he is pictured knocking at the church's door – but concerned not only for the church as a whole, but for each individual Christian who belongs to his church. This is clear from the words he uses: 'If anyone hears my voice and opens the door, I will come in to him and dine with him, and he with me.'

How does the Lord Jesus Christ knock, in his ministry of rebuking and chastening those whom he loves, in order to prepare such for heaven? He knocks with his Word. Every time you read it, every time you hear it preached, every time you meditate upon it, Christ knocks upon your mind, your heart, your soul and your conscience. He knocks with his blessings of godly parents and Christian friends, not least when they are taken away. He knocks with his ministers (the stars in his right hand, 1:20) who seek to deal faithfully with your souls as men who have to give an account. He knocks with his providences – the sweet ones, as overwhelming tokens of his goodness and mercy to dissolve you in thankfulness and turn you to praise, and the dark ones, just as much. In all that he sends to you and in all that he withholds from you, in what he grants you and in what he denies you, he is knocking. In this connection, Robert Murray M'Cheyne remarked, 'I always feel in much need of God's afflicting hand'; and John 'Rabbi' Duncan observed, 'If we have not got a cross, alas! we may conclude that we have not Christ, for it is the first of his gifts.'

4 To what purposes does he do this?

We have considered the one great over-arching and over-ruling purpose: to prepare us for heaven. Yet with that always in view: to what subsidiary ends does the Lord deal with us in his rebukes, chastenings and disciplines? You can group the answer to that question under the twin headings of 'things to get rid of from us' and 'things to increase in us'. There are all too many dangers and snares confronting us in the Christian life (some of which we are aware, others not so obvious) against which we need to be guarded, warned and kept. Think of some in either category.

There are those things which need to be got rid of. They need to go. They are bad lodgers and need not only to be given notice to quit but actually to be evicted. Such as? All those things which are 'of the earth' or 'earthy'. Some of them come to mind immediately. There is our greater love for other people or other things rather than a pure devotion to Christ alone; our distrust and mistrust of God's ways and provisions; our sin of pride, smugness, sinful boasting (compare 3:17, and the Laodiceans' bloated view of themselves: 'I am rich, have become wealthy, and have need of nothing') which inevitably leads to lukewarmness in the things of God (as it did with them); our slothfulness, idleness and lack of concern for the interests of Christ's kingdom (have a look at Philippians 2:21); our attraction (still) to the things of the flesh and the sinful nature; our worldliness, our love of the world and the things and honours of the world – and so the list goes on. Enough said?

There are also those things which need to increase in us. Such as? All those things which are 'from above' or 'heavenly'. Some of them also come to mind immediately. There are the Christlike virtues of the fruit of the Spirit; faith strengthened, believing the promises and walking by faith, not by sight; a closer and better knowledge of God, and contentment with everything about him; a richer fruitfulness in our lives which never fails to give to God alone all the glory and never keeps any of it back for ourselves; a heavenly- and holy-mindedness, genuinely longing to be gone – and, once again, so the list goes on. Enough said?

Ryle has this to say when speaking of God's people passing through tribulations and suffering the sting of affliction. 'It is their Father's hand which chastens them; it is thus he weans their affection from things below and fixes them on himself; it is thus he trains them for eternity, and cuts the threads one by one which bind their wavering hearts to earth. No doubt such chastening is grievous for the time, but still it brings many a hidden grace to light, and cuts down many a secret seed of evil; and we shall see those who have suffered most shining among the brightest stars in the assembly of heaven. The purest gold is that which has been longest in the refiner's furnace. The brightest diamond is often that which has required the most grinding and polishing.'[24]

All of this, then, with heaven in view. Never forget that! In such ways our God prepares us for heaven. It will mean some sighing and some groaning as his tools are at work upon us: his hammer and his chisel, and the like. But do not despise it. Do not murmur against it. Do not faint under it. Listen to Thomas Boston (who knew the subject of this chapter from deep personal experience): 'it is the usual way of providence with me that blessing comes through several iron gates.' Does it seem to be like that with you, too, at least at times?

God would have himself to be your all – your portion for ever. He knows (in perfect wisdom, abounding grace and perfect divine love) all that it takes, exactly what is needful, to reach that end, and is determined to bring you, if you are his own true child, safe to glory, well prepared for that glory.

In the light of all this, a closing word might be in order on the matter of our response to these often difficult and mysterious experiences. We are neither to despise the Lord's dealings with us nor despair under them. Thomas Brooks has a treatise with the memorable title *The Mute Christian under the Smarting Rod*. It is to be found in the first volume of his works. He sums up the doctrine he is treating as follows: 'That it is the great duty and concernment of gracious souls to be mute and silent under the greatest afflictions, the saddest providences, and sharpest trials that they meet with in this world.' In other words, we are not to murmur or complain; we are not to become hard-hearted or insensitive; we are not to accuse God or faint and give up; we are not to grow careless or become too quick to speak.

One of the questions he raises is, 'what doth a prudent, a gracious, a holy silence include?' It would be profitable to record here how he answers that. He writes, 'it includes and takes in these eight things':

1 A sight of God, and an acknowledgment of God as the author of all the afflictions that come upon us

2 Some holy, gracious apprehensions of the majesty, sovereignty, dignity, authority, and presence of that God under whose afflicting hand we are

3 A holy quietness and calmness of mind and spirit, under the afflicting hand

4 An humble, justifying, clearing and acquitting of God of all blame, rigour and injustice, in all the afflictions he brings upon us

5 Gracious, blessed, soul-quieting conclusions about the issue and event of those afflictions that are upon us (such as that they shall work for our good, keep us humble and low, and will not always lie upon us)

6 A strict charge, a solemn command, that conscience lays upon the soul to be quiet and still

7 A surrendering, a resigning up of ourselves to God, whilst we are under his afflicting hand

8 A patient waiting upon the Lord under our afflictions until deliverance comes.

We come back, of course, to the Lord's clear and firm assertion, 'As many as *I love*, I rebuke and chasten.' God punishes his enemies as their Judge; he chastens his children as their Father. He takes vengeance upon his foes; he disciplines those whom he has redeemed. His punishing of sinners honours his law and vindicates his government; his chastising of his children is for their spiritual well-being and to prepare them for heaven. Linking in with our much earlier chapter on the purity of heaven, and the principle established there of 'no holiness – no heaven', this remark from William Gurnall is appropriate here: 'God would not rub so hard if it were not to fetch out the dirt that is ingrained in our natures. God loves purity so well he had rather see a hole than a spot in his child's garments.' So let our response be the response of spiritual men and women as we look in faith to the blessed issue and outcome of it all.

> With mercy and with judgement
> My web of time He wove,
> And aye the dews of sorrow
> Were lustred with His love:
> I'll bless the hand that guided,
> I'll bless the heart that planned,
> When throned where glory dwelleth
> In Immanuel's land.
>
> Anne Ross Cousin.

Thomas Charles on the preparation for heaven

Thomas Charles (1755-1814) was born in South Wales, and was converted under the ministry of Daniel Rowland at Llangeitho. His ministry in Wales began in 1784 and was focused in the north of the country. The name of Bala is permanently associated with him. He became the leader of the Calvinistic Methodists, and lived to witness a remarkable season of spiritual awakening.

As well as much preaching, he was also engaged in the establishing of 'circulating schools', by which pattern a school would be set up in a place for some six to nine months, during which time the young people would be taught to read the Scriptures, after which the schoolmaster would move elsewhere and do the same thing there; the formation of Sunday schools, such that he has been described as 'one of the most successful leaders of children's work of all time'; and the publishing of Christian literature to aid in the study of Scripture, including a quarterly magazine called *The Spiritual Treasury* and his major four-volume work, a *Scriptural Dictionary*. He laboured extensively at the work of the printing and distributing of the Welsh Bible, and a well-known account records how a sixteen-year old girl, Mary Jones, after saving up her money carefully for as long as it took, walked barefoot the thirty miles to Charles' home in Bala in 1800 to buy a Bible. It was said of him that he lived 'with heaven in his face'.

Among his 'essays, letters and papers' is a piece entitled *Affliction*, which, in a most spiritual and practical manner, deals with the use and benefits thereof. The following is an extract from it, bearing very much upon this subject we have been considering of the preparation for heaven.[25]

'"Affliction cometh not forth out of the dust, neither doth trouble spring out of the ground": but they are all sent in wisdom and love; and every circumstance, as to time and manner, is exactly ordered for the best. Were every circumstance more widely examined, it would doubtless give us a great insight into the wisdom and love of God in all his afflictive dispensations. God doth not willingly afflict any of his children: but they always stand in absolute need, at the very time, of the very affliction which he sends. It could not be laid aside, nor delayed, nor altered for another, without great hurt and injury to the soul.

God's designs in afflictions are various; but all gracious, and for our good. He may intend to bring us to repentance for some past sins, as the three days' pestilence was sent to humble David for numbering the people; or, it may be to prevent our being taken in some dangerous snare, into which we may be in great danger of falling: and it is better to endure the heaviest affliction, than to carry about with us a guilty conscience. 'Any thing rather than sin', is the language of the Christian's heart. Or it may be to exercise some grace, that it may thereby gain strength, and the soul be prepared for some trying circumstance into which it is soon to be brought; as was the case with Joseph. The trials with which he had been exercised, prepared him for his future exaltation, and some of them contributed to bring it about.

These designs may for a long season be concealed from the believer himself, as was the case with Joseph. Yet, inasmuch as God hath assured us, that all things shall work together for good, patience and resignation to the divine will in all things is our duty. In his good time he may give us to see such wisdom and goodness in all, as to fill our hearts with transports of joy. To follow him is our part, without murmuring, without complaining. How gracious is the design to bring us to repentance for sin, or to stop us from falling into temptation, or to prepare us by previous discipline for some humbling service! Is not all this good? Away then with all impatience and all murmurings. Nothing befalls us without a cause: and no trouble comes upon us sooner, or presses more heavily, or continues longer, than our case requires. What our shortsighted ignorance calls adversities or evils, are in reality and truth, well-designed and gracious blessings, and form a part of the means employed by God's goodness and grace to prepare us for the exceeding and eternal weight of glory.

All our desire in this world should be to live holily and live usefully: and affliction, by the blessing of God, hath great influence in promoting both. It greatly promotes holiness, and is also no small preparative for usefulness. It is working out at the same time a far more exceeding and eternal weight of glory in the other world. God always chastens us for our profit. Though we may thereby lose earthly comforts, ease, and enjoyments; yet it is a profitable loss. What we lose in these things, we gain in holiness. It is for our profit, to become partakers of his holiness. It is for our profit, to be brought to repentance for every sin, to be delivered from ensnaring temptations, or to be prepared for any service to which our master may call us. If we cannot see the end the Lord hath in view, still let us believe, that it is for our profit in some way or other, yes, and in the way of all others, by which we can profit the most, and be the greatest gainers.'

9

THE MARRIAGE IN HEAVEN

We are familiar with the announcement 'a marriage has been arranged', and with being asked the question 'will you be at the wedding?'. There is a very special marriage – indeed an absolutely unique wedding – spoken of in the book of Revelation, and we come now to consider it. It has already been arranged. In fact, those arrangements were laid even before the creation of the world. Back in eternity, the Father made a choice of a people and gave them to his Son. The Lord Jesus Christ himself has this in mind when he says, 'All that the Father gives me will come to me, and the one who comes to me I will by no means cast out' (John 6:37). It is this very arrangement which is brought to its high and ultimate end on that day spoken of in the portion of Revelation we are about to consider, when the Lord Jesus Christ takes to himself everlastingly those whom his Father gave to him from of old. Everything is ready, all at tremendous cost and trouble, and with no expense spared. But will you be there?

This marriage in heaven is set forth in 19:7-9. 'Let us be glad and rejoice and give him glory, for the marriage of the Lamb has come, and his wife has made herself ready', is how that section starts. Do you see there the name given to this marriage? It is the marriage or wedding of the Lamb, and we know already from some of our earlier chapters that 'the Lamb' refers to only one person: the Lord Jesus Christ. So this is his marriage. This is his wedding day. No wonder it is such a special occasion. Spurgeon is correct to say that 'it is divinely veiled as well as revealed' here in Revelation, and he goes on to remark, 'God forbid that we should intrude where the Holy Spirit shuts us out; but still, what we do know of it, let us now think upon, and may the sacred Spirit make it profitable to us.'[26]

However, so that we can see this marriage in its most glorious light, we must first of all go back a little in Revelation 19 and begin by noticing:

The solemn prelude to the marriage

It is usually the case that before any really important event, whatever that event might be, there are things leading up to it. Certain things take place beforehand. There are things that are preludes to 'the big event' and that usher it in. Well, so it is in the present case, as the earlier verses of chapter 19 make clear. In fact, there are two highly significant events which are a prelude to the marriage of the Lamb. The first is the complete destruction of the false church. The second is the glorious outpouring of praise to God. A word on each would be in place.

First, *the complete destruction of the false church*. Chapters 17 and 18 of Revelation have already recorded the fall of Babylon and featured a vision given to the apostle John of an appalling looking woman, all painted up and flashed up gaudily and offensively. Look back to 17:3-5.

Now, what is Babylon all about? In summary: Babylon represents the world with all its seductions and charms; everything which seeks to allure and draw people away from God; everything which plays upon 'the lust of the flesh, the lust of the eyes, and the pride of life' (1 John 2:16). That is not all. There is more: the endless false representations of the Gospel; the cults, the church of Rome, the ecumenical movement; the alliance between church and state, the church and the world, which ends up blurring the distinctiveness between the two. Revelation 17 and 18, along with some of the earlier chapters as well, present a terrible picture of the false church, the apostate church, following Satan's deceits and lies, rebelling against the living God and his truth, perverting the only true Gospel, committing fornication with the kings and princes and powers of the world, and seeking to build its own kingdom which has nothing whatsoever to do with the spiritual kingdom of the Lord Jesus Christ.

There are two churches in the world, however much folk refuse to acknowledge it, or are blind to it. There is the true church (called of God and separated unto him, composed of those who have been chosen from eternity, born of the Holy Spirit, washed in Christ's blood for the forgiveness of their sins, and who cleave to the truth of his Word in every part). And there is the false church (which is none of those things, even though it 'poses' as if it is, and is taken by many to be the real thing). The true church is often (though not always) small and despised. The false church is often (though not always) popular and acclaimed – but her sins are rising up to heaven and her doom and punishment are inevitable, and will be sudden, final and complete.

Second, *the great outpouring of praise to God*. There are no less than four 'Alleluias' in the opening verses of Revelation 19: verses 1,3,4,6, where the praises of God are set forth not only because in and of himself he is worthy of praise (for he is God) but because of what is recorded at the end of verse 1 and through verse 2. 'Salvation and glory and honour and power to the Lord our God! For true and righteous are his judgments, because he has judged the great prostitute who corrupted the earth with her fornication; and he has avenged on her the blood of his servants shed by her.'

The judgment of Babylon, the world, the false church, is the vindication of God, the vindication of the gospel, the vindication of God's own people. So how he is to be praised! Just as Babylon's glory and prosperity had been the joy of the world and the grief of the children of God, so her downfall is the joy of God's people and the ruin of the kingdom of unbelief. Hence the Alleluias – for what he has done, for the glory of his name.

There is a remarkable sermon of M'Cheyne entitled *The Eternal Torment of the Wicked matter of Eternal Song to the Redeemed*. In considering 'the reason why the redeemed will rejoice at the condemnation of the wicked', the preacher declares 'it is not because they love to see human pain', and 'it is not because they will see the destruction of their enemies'. What then is the reason (for this subject has often presented something of a 'difficulty', as it were, for some Christians)? The reason, says M'Cheyne, is: 'in one word, it is because the redeemed will have no mind but God's. They will have no joy but what the Lord has .... Now the redeemed will be of the same mind with God when they get to heaven. And God must change his nature before he can quench the fire of hell.' I do commend the whole sermon to you as most worthy of your careful and prayerful perusal.[27]

It is worthy of notice that in verse 5 we read the following. 'Then a voice came from the throne, saying, "Praise our God, all you his servants and those who fear him, both small and great!"' The very call itself to praise God proceeds 'from the throne', and it is couched in terms of 'Praise *our* God'. Taking the spokesman to be the Lord Jesus Christ himself, what a glimpse it gives us of how close he is to his people, even though exalted to the highest place. It is an indication of his love for us, his condescension towards us, his identification with us, and that he is not ashamed of us. He is, most certainly, our Kinsman-Redeemer. We are reminded of his words in Hebrews 2:12: 'I will declare your name to my brethren; in the midst of the congregation I will sing praise to you'; and again, in the following verse, 'Here am I and the children whom God has given me.' It is the Mediator himself who issues the call to praise not 'your God' but 'our God'. In the heavenly places, we shall not only praise the Lamb, but be led in praise by the Lamb. Think of that!

All of this means that the scene is set for the magnificent announcement of verse 7, that 'the marriage of the Lamb has come, and his wife has made herself ready.'

The happy couple at the marriage
Both a bridegroom and a bride are essential to a wedding. You cannot have a marriage without them. (That, incidentally, is not intended as a facetious point. The thinking, and, increasingly, the practice of the world, with support from the false church, is that two bridegrooms or two brides will do just as well. Such is an abomination to God. There must be one bridegroom and one bride). So at this marriage, as you would expect, both bridegroom and bride are mentioned (and, notice, in that order, for since the Lord Jesus Christ, the Lamb, is the bridegroom, he must 'in all things ... have the pre-eminence' (Col. 1:18)).

Look first, then, at *the bridegroom*. Attention was drawn earlier in this book to the appropriateness of this name 'the Lamb' for the Lord Jesus Christ. It places the emphasis upon his work as the sinner's Saviour. He is 'the Lamb slain from the foundation of the world' (Rev. 13:8), 'the Lamb of God who takes away the sin of the world' (John 1:29), 'a lamb without blemish and without spot' (1 Pet. 1:19), who shed his 'precious blood' on the cross at Calvary. He died there as a sacrificial victim, as the substitute in the sinner's place, as 'the just for the unjust, that he might bring us to God' (1 Pet. 3:18). How lovely the Lord Jesus Christ is in every respect; but how especially and supremely lovely he is to those who love him in his character as the Lamb! How it reveals his glory. How it manifests his love. As the Lamb, 'Christ ... loved the church and gave himself up for it' (Eph. 5:25).

> From heaven He came and sought her
> To be His holy bride;
> With His own blood he bought her,
> And for her life He died.

S J Stone

How striking it is that this blessed union between the Lord and his church is so specifically denoted as 'the marriage of the Lamb'. Here is Spurgeon again. 'The ever blessed and eternal union of hearts with Christ will be in reference to his sacrifice ... Jesus Christ as the Lamb, the sacrifice, is not only the beginning, but the end; not only the foundation, but the topstone of the whole sacred edifice of the temple of grace. The consummation of the whole work of redemption is the marriage of the church to Christ.'

Then look at *the bride*. There is no question as to her identity. The bride of the Lamb is the church of Christ. The church is pictured here as one bride (v. 7, the church as a whole) and many guests (v. 9, believers considered individually). John

'Rabbi' Duncan remarked, 'Next to the sight of the Lamb, I would like to see his bride.' What bride does not want to look her very best on her wedding day? The reason for that, very especially, is to please her bridegroom. So it is with the bride of the Lamb. How beautiful she will be. Look at verse 7b: 'and his wife has made herself ready'.

This, however, is not some do-it-yourself beauty treatment. Look on to verse 8: 'And to her it was granted to be arrayed in fine linen.' Notice the emphasis on 'granted' (or 'given'). Someone has remarked: 'He (the Lamb) decks and dresses his own bride with the ornaments of grace here and glory hereafter.' Is that not choice? What do we have of ourselves? Nothing at all. What do we have through, from and in the Lord Jesus Christ? Absolutely everything! There is in him all the righteousness we need – both imputed righteousness (in salvation, as the righteousness of Christ himself is, as it were, charged to our account, and freely given to us), and imparted righteousness (in sanctification, as the Lord Jesus Christ is formed in us, and we become increasingly like him as a result of the work of the Holy Spirit both within us and upon us).

Observe verse 8 in full. 'And to her it was granted to be arrayed in fine linen, clean and bright, for the fine linen represents the righteous acts (or, righteousnesses) of the saints.' It is a statement and a picture of the bride availed of her husband's own righteousness in glory. It speaks of the bride prepared, the bride made ready. Everything about *her* draws attention and brings glory to *him*.

All of this is very redolent of Psalm 45, in which is set forth the glories of the Messiah and his bride. It is a wedding psalm which declares first of all, in the most magnificent manner, the fairness, graciousness, majesty, righteousness, gladness and fragrance of Christ, the royal bridegroom; and then proceeds to relish, in a sumptuous manner, the loveliness of his bride and her delight in and delight to her husband. 'So the King will greatly desire your beauty; because he is your Lord, worship him ... She shall be brought to the King in robes of many colours; the virgins, her companions who follow her, shall be brought to you. With gladness and rejoicing they shall be brought; they shall enter the King's palace' (Ps. 45:11, 14-15).

Think of it this way, if it is helpful. At present the Lord Jesus Christ has but a poor reward for all his sufferings. His people seem few, feeble and scattered; afflicted and scarred in endless ways. Yet when he takes his bride to himself on his wedding day, she will be as pure, as beautiful, as holy and as resplendent as you can imagine – or, indeed, as she could ever possibly be. Never will there have been such a bridegroom. Equally, never will there have been such a bride. For when *he* appears, *she* will appear also, and she will be like him in his glory (remember 1 John 3:2). What a prospect for the church, and what an assurance for believers. Furthermore, fundamental to the church's union with Christ (as bride and bridegroom) is the reality of the church's own unity within herself. That also is part of the readiness spoken of here. For this the bridegroom himself prayed: 'that they may be one as we (the Father and the Son) are', 'that they all may be one, as you, Father, are in me, and I in you; that they also may be one in us' (John 17:11,21).

'Now to him who is able to keep you from stumbling, and to present you faultless before the presence of his glory with exceeding joy, to God our Saviour, who alone is wise, be glory and majesty, dominion and power, both now and for ever. Amen' (Jude 24-25).

One thing, though: is the church not already married to Christ? Yes – indeed she is. But it is rather like the pattern of Jewish wedding ceremonies. The bridegroom and the bride would become 'betrothed' to one another (not like our 'engagement', which can be an 'on and off' affair, but more equivalent to a marriage itself in its binding and exclusive nature). Next, the couple would live separately from one another for a season (though belonging to one another). Then, finally, the bridegroom would return to take his bride to his own home, and the marriage supper would follow and their married life proceed.

Can you see the parallel? Donald MacDonald works it out a little as follows. 'As we go through this life as a Christian church our Bridegroom is absent. He married us to Himself and then He went away. He went away to the palace, to the mansion of His Father, and He left us in this world to fight the conflicts of life, the good fight of faith, to wage the warfare of the Christian. He left us to tread in His footsteps, but we do not see Him, we have never seen Him. The vale of time is between us. We see Him by faith, but we have never seen Him with our natural eyes. But there, we shall see Him face to face, and His name shall be in our foreheads.'[28]

The eternal blessedness of the marriage

The picture of the marriage supper or wedding feast continues in verse 9 of our present portion. Often (in the picture I have just given above of wedding customs) the feast would last for a full week, or even two. The marriage feast of the heavenly Lamb and his glorious bride, however, truly lasts for ever. This is a love without end. This really is living happily ever after. This is rejoicing for evermore.

This is a union which is perfect. If ever a marriage was made in heaven (as the saying goes) this is the one! This is a day which lasts for ever. This is a happiness which never ceases. The bridegroom and his bride will be completely taken up with one another for ever, with nothing to spoil, nothing to grow stale, nothing to cause tension, and nothing to separate them or come between them in any way.

Occasionally on earth marriages are announced that never take place. Wedding invitations are issued which have to be cancelled or withdrawn. Preparations are made which never materialise. Everything falls through. Or there are occasions where, even when the marriage takes place, it does not last, but comes to an end in some kind of grief or other. Moreover, even the best and happiest of earthly marriages have to end sometime in bereavement, anyway. In contrast to all of this, however, meditate upon the privilege of being married to the Lamb, united to Christ, gathered to him, embraced by him, loved by him and being with him *for ever*. Like Ruth of old (Ruth 1:9; 4:11), the church will find rest in the house of her husband.

Again, on earth (especially with 'royal' or 'society' weddings) you hear them described as 'the wedding of the year', or some other grand claim is made for them. But they are of the earth. Yet, again in stark contrast, the marriage of the Lamb is the marriage in heaven. This marriage alone has the right to be spoken of as *'the marriage'*, not only of the year but of all time. There will never have been anything like it before – and, of necessity, there can never be one like it afterwards.

Does all of this seem too good to be true? And does the thought of you having a part in it seem too good to be true? Do you sometimes wonder if it will ever really happen? To

this very point, here is another helpful paragraph from
Donald MacDonald to help us in the business of assurance.
'You are afraid that the ring you wear is not His gift; you are
afraid that the dress you have on is not His righteousness;
you are afraid that the marriage certificate has not been signed
by Him, and therefore is not valid. But banish your fears,
banish them all. The ring you have *is* His, He gave it to you.
He put it on your finger. Who else could put it on? And the
dress you wear is His righteousness, clean and white. Who
else had it to give you? This is the marriage dress woven by
Him with hands imbrued with blood, His pierced hands. Oh
what a precious garment it is! Who else could give you a
garment like it? Who else could give you a garment, won
and paid for by substitution, by being forsaken by the Father
on the cross? Do not be afraid; trust fully in your Lord. His
name is on your certificate also, as well as your own. His
name is on it as sure and surer even than yours and if your
name is on it, it is because His name was on it first. And at
the feast we shall see Him.'[29]

So, will you be there?

How can you know?

The test is really a very simple and obvious one. If you
would belong to the Lord Jesus Christ on his wedding day
described in our text, you must belong to him now. If you
would be married to the Lamb, you must belong to the Lamb.
That means: you must be trusting him as your Saviour from
sin now. You must be honouring him as the Lord of your life
now. You must be desiring to be like him in his holiness
now. You must be acknowledging and confessing his name
and so being on the Lord's side now. You must be delighting
in him, taken up with him, obeying him and following him
now. You must be longing for him and for his appearing

now. If you are not, it is no use you fooling yourself that you are a Christian. And if you are not a Christian, it is no use imagining you will be united to Christ on the day of his marriage. Rather, instead of him saying to you, 'Come to me', he will say to you, 'Depart from me.' Instead of you hearing his voice saying, 'You are mine', you will hear him saying, 'I never knew you.'

Think carefully. Will the marriage in heaven be the best day of your life, as you are gathered in to the Lord Jesus Christ for ever? Or will it be the worst day of your life, as you are separated from him for ever?

'Then he said to me, "Write: 'Blessed are those who are called to the marriage supper of the Lamb!'" And he said to me, "These are the true sayings of God."'

> Midst the darkness, storm and sorrow
> One bright gleam I see;
> Well I know the blessed morrow –
> Christ will come for me.
>
> Midst the light and peace and glory
> Of the Father's home,
> Christ for me is watching, waiting,
> Waiting till I come.
>
> Oh, the blessed joy of meeting –
> All the desert past:
> Oh, the wondrous words of greeting
> He shall speak at last!
>
> He and I in that bright glory
> One deep joy shall share:
> Mine, to be for ever with Him,
> His, that I am there!

Gerhard Tersteegen.

Samuel Rutherford on the marriage in heaven

Samuel Rutherford (1600-1661) is the obvious one to help us in this lovely matter of the marriage in heaven between Christ and his bride. How full of Christ Rutherford was, and how full and overflowing his famous letters are on this subject. The godly pastor of 'fair Anwoth by the Solway' was exiled for almost two years to Aberdeen ('Christ's Palace in Aberdeen', as he called it), where, in days of great tension between church and state, he was prohibited from preaching and had to endure what he poignantly referred to as 'dumb Sabbaths'. In 1643 he travelled to London as one of the Scottish commissioners to the Westminster Assembly of Divines.

A choice account survives of the experience of an English merchant on the occasion of a visit he made, first to Irvine and then to St Andrews (where in 1639 Rutherford became a Professor). This man records, 'I came to Irvine, and heard a well-favoured, proper old man (David Dickson), with a long beard, and that man showed me all my heart. Then I went to St Andrews, where I heard a sweet, majestic-looking man (Robert Blair), and he showed me the majesty of God. After him I heard a little, fair man (Samuel Rutherford) and he showed me the loveliness of Christ.'

Rutherford described himself as 'hungry in waiting for the marriage supper of the Lamb'. Two of his biographers record that his last words were, 'Glory, glory dwelleth in Immanuel's land.' While his writings were several, it is his *Letters* for which he remains best known and loved by those who are devoted to Christ. Many of them were written during his banishment in Aberdeen. Spurgeon regarded them as 'the nearest thing to inspiration which can be found in the writings of mere men'. They were written to a whole company of correspondents and exhibit a most remarkable spirituality, warmth, devotion, pastoral tenderness, faithfulness to the gospel, and concern for 'Christ's crown and covenant'.[30]

There is an abundance of allusion in these letters to the marriage of the Lamb, with Rutherford often using language which is redolent of the Old Testament book, the Song of Songs. Here are several choice extracts which bear upon our present theme.

'I dare not challenge Himself (ie, Christ), but His absence is a mountain of iron upon my heavy heart. Oh, when shall we meet? Oh, how long is it to the dawning of the marriage-day? O sweet Lord Jesus, take wide steps! O my Lord, come over mountains at one stride! O my Beloved, be like a roe or a young hart on the mountains of Separation (Song 2:17). Oh, if He would fold the heavens together like an old cloak, and shovel time and days out of the way, and make ready in haste the Lamb's wife for her Husband! Since He looked upon me, my heart is not mine own; He hath run away to heaven with it.'

'O how sweet to be wholly Christ's, and wholly in Christ; to dwell in Immanuel's high and blessed land, and live in that sweetest air, where no wind bloweth but the breathings of the Holy Ghost, no sea nor floods flow but the pure water of life that floweth from under the throne and from the Lamb, no planting but the tree of life that yieldeth twelve manner of fruits every month! What do we here but sin and suffer? O when shall the night be gone, the shadows flee away, and the morning of the long, long day, without cloud or night, dawn? The Spirit and the bride say, 'Come!' O, when shall the Lamb's wife be ready, and the Bridegroom say, 'Come'?'

He mentions in one letter that God 'hath now let me see four things which I never saw before', the first of which is:

'That the Supper shall be great cheer, that is up in the great hall with the Royal King of glory ... When He bloweth a kiss afar off to His poor heart-broken mourners in Zion, and sendeth me but His hearty commendations till we meet, I am confounded with wonder to think what it shall be, when the Fairest among the sons of men shall lay a King's sweet soft cheek to the sinful cheeks of poor sinners.'

'O for the coming of the Bridegroom! Oh, when shall I see the Bridegroom and the Bride meet in the clouds, and kiss each other! Oh, when will we get our day, and our heart's fill of that love! Oh, if it were lawful to complain of the famine of that love, and want of the immediate vision of God!'

'The great Angel of the covenant bear you company, till the trumpet shall sound, and the voice of the Archangel awaken the dead. Ye shall find it your only happiness, under whatever thing disturbeth and crosseth the peace of your mind, in this life, to love nothing for itself, but only God for Himself. It is the crooked love of some harlots, that they love bracelets, ear-rings, and rings better than the lover that sendeth them. God will not so be loved; for that were to behave as harlots, and not as the chaste spouse, to abate from our love when these things are pulled away. Our love to Him should begin on earth, as it shall be in heaven; for the bride taketh not, by a thousand degrees, so much delight in her wedding garment as she doth in her bridegroom; so we, in the life to come, howbeit clothed with glory as with a robe, shall not be so much affected with the glory that goeth about us, as with the bridegroom's joyful face and presence.'

10

THE INVITATION TO HEAVEN

Why did the Lord Jesus Christ come down to earth from heaven? He did so in order to take his people back with him from earth to heaven. He came to seek and to save lost sinners, to call and gather them to himself, and to deliver them safely to heaven, so that where he now is, we may be also. It is not surprising, therefore, to find that there are many gracious invitations recorded in the Bible – invitations from God to us, from the Saviour to sinners, and so we turn our attention next in our consideration of the doctrine of heaven in the book of Revelation to what I am calling the invitation to heaven. Nowhere in the book is it found more richly or exquisitely than in 22:17: 'And the Spirit and the bride say, "Come!" And let him who hears say, "Come!" And let him who thirsts come. And whoever desires, let him take the water of life freely.'

The question arises as to the precise interpretation of this verse. Is the whole of it an invitation, such that the Spirit (the Holy Spirit), the bride (the whole church of Christ) and 'him who hears' (the individual saved sinner) are all issuing the invitation to 'him who thirsts' to come and 'take the water of life freely'? Or is their united 'Come!' a longing addressed to the Lord Jesus Christ for his return – he who has already announced back in verse 7, 'Behold, I am coming quickly!' (compare also verse 20) – with then an invitation at the end of the verse to thirsty souls to 'take the water of life freely', that they also will be moved to utter this same cry to Christ of 'Come!'? Students of the book of Revelation differ upon this. Either way, however, the gospel invitation in the second part of the verse is a very clear and genuine one to needy souls. Ultimately, of course, as the gospel is proclaimed, as the work of evangelism prospers and as God's irresistible grace presses the word of grace home, it is the Saviour himself who is calling sinners to himself. If this were not so, you might well doubt the sheer magnificence of such an invitation as we find here. But such doubt should have no place at all. We shall proceed by noticing in turn three features of this invitation which merit special attention.

How gracious it is

This can be seen in a number of different ways. In the first place, *the invitation speaks of a free gift*. 'And whoever desires, let him take the water of life freely.' NIV translates that as 'the free gift of the water of life', which underscores the point, though 'let him take the water of life freely' is the correct and literal translation. So here is a free gift. It is not a deserved one (as the payment of wages due); nor a merited one (earned for good behaviour or character); nor an obliged one (due to us or owed to us for any reason). It is an absolutely free gift of which the Lord Jesus Christ speaks.

Are you suspicious of free gifts? Where have they come from? If someone appears to be giving something away, do you wonder automatically what is wrong with it? Do you imagine there must be a catch somewhere? There is no need for suspicion here. Indeed, it would be insulting and offensive to the Son of God who, remember, is the one offering this free gift.

There is another well-known and much-loved Bible verse which speaks along the same lines. 'Ho! Everyone who thirsts, come to the waters; and you who have no money, come, buy and eat. Yes, come, buy wine and milk without money and without price' (Isa. 55:1).

In the second place, *the invitation is offered to needy ones*. Take special notice of the phrase, 'him who thirsts'. You see the same in the Isaiah verse just quoted.

What do thirsty people need? Water. What does that water do? It quenches their thirst. It meets and satisfies their need, which may often be an extreme one (especially if the day or climate is exceedingly hot, or if they have had to go without water for a long time). Thirst is dangerous. You can, quite literally, die of thirst. But it is spiritual things that are being spoken of here in Revelation 22: spiritual water to quench spiritual thirst, spiritual provision to meet spiritual need, spiritual life to save you from spiritual death.

Then, in the third place, *the invitation focuses upon the very thing which thirsty souls need*. What is this water of life which you are bidden to take freely? It is God's gift of salvation through his Son, the Lord Jesus Christ – nothing less than that. To describe it a little more fully: it is pardon for guilty sinners. It is peace with God for those who by nature are rebels against him. It is eternal life for those who are heading for judgment and condemnation and everlasting torment. It is a home in heaven for those whose sins are otherwise taking them to hell. Another delightful verse in Isaiah speaks of drawing water from the wells of salvation, and doing so with joy (Isa. 12:3). It is a similar picture. Here it is thirsty souls, needy sinners, taking God's gift of the water of life freely.

What does the Lord Jesus Christ say himself? Remember his conversation with the Samaritan woman at the well. 'Jesus answered and said to her, "Whoever drinks of this water (ie, referring to the ordinary water in the well) will thirst again, but whoever drinks of the water that I shall give him (ie, speaking now of spiritual and heavenly things) will never thirst. But the water that I shall give him will become in him a fountain of water springing up into everlasting life"' (John 4:13-14).

Sinner: you need Christ! You need him to save you from your sins. You need him to bring you to God. You need him to take you to heaven. You are lost, helpless and hopeless without him. He is the one – and he alone is the one – whom God the Father has graciously provided for thirsty souls. From him – and from him alone – you may receive an abundant supply of everything you can ever possibly need for the relief of all your soul's needs, just as from an abundant, ever-flowing or over-flowing stream.

As you and I are in ourselves: we die, we perish, we sink into the depths of hell. As we may become in Christ by grace: we live, we rise, we ascend to the very heights of heaven.

How generous it is

Focus upon the second part of 22:17. 'And let him who thirsts come. And whoever desires, let him take the water of life freely.' First there is the 'let him who thirsts', which is then immediately followed by the 'and whoever desires'. A literal translation reads particularly strikingly and beautifully: 'the thirsting one, let him come; the wishing one, let him take the water of life freely.' Could anything read more generously?

The invitation is to 'the thirsting one': 'let him who thirsts come.' It is to 'the wishing one': 'And whoever desires, let him take the water of life freely.'

Behold the bounty, the generosity and the abundance of God to sinners. It is not a case of 'whoever is clever, whoever is wealthy, whoever is famous'; nor is it 'whoever understands everything, whoever feels all that they should feel, whoever has been brought up in a particular way'; and it is most certainly not 'whoever is worthy, whoever is deserving, whoever has come up to a certain standard'. It is simply (though profoundly) this: 'let him who thirsts come', 'whoever desires, let him take the water of life freely'. The terms could not possibly be more generous. Someone has put it vividly: 'there is no standard-height here. It is of any height and any size. Little sinners, big sinners, black sinners, fair sinners, sinners double dyed, old sinners, aggravated sinners, sinners who have committed every crime in the whole catalogue.' It is 'whoever'. This is the free offer of the gospel indeed! It addresses you, dear reader, whoever you are and whatever you are – and whatever you have been.

How welcome it is
It should be welcome, anyway. But is it? Is it welcome to you as you read it?

A prior question, of course, is this: are you thirsty? And are you wishing? For it is the thirsty who come and drink and are satisfied. It is those desirous of it, longing for it, desperate for it, who do not need inviting twice to 'take the water of life freely', to drink it 'without money and without price', and to go on drinking as from a well without stint or measure. These are the ones who, having discovered the Lord Jesus Christ (or, better, having been found by him, for that is always the true way that it is), go on drinking from him, enjoying him, delighting in him and being satisfied in him for ever, and who find in heaven itself, when life in this vale of tears is over, that in his presence is 'fullness of joy', and at his right hand are 'pleasures for evermore' (Ps. 16:11).

How welcome this invitation is, therefore, to thirsty, desiring souls. But I press the question: is this an accurate and appropriate description of you? Are you thirsty? Are you desiring? Would you come? Would you drink? Would you take freely? For this is no mirage in the desert. This is no false trail.

While the majority of people who might ever read this book are likely to be Christians already, the subject of heaven holds such fascination sometimes even for those who are not Christians that I am hopeful and prayerful as I write these lines that some who do not as yet belong to the Lord Jesus Christ will find their way to reading these pages. Now, in particular, is the moment when I must 'speak' with you.

I ask you yet again: are you thirsty? are you wishing? I fear lest you are not – lest, even as you have read thus far (and maybe you have read a number of 'Christian books') you have never really known a true spiritual longing for God. Maybe there have been odd times when certain impressions were made upon your soul, but they all passed off. They took their course. And even though you have continued to read, to think about things, and perhaps to attend under the preaching of God's Word in church, it is still without any real desire to know God, still with no conscious sense of how much you need him, still without any urgent longing to have your sin dealt with, and still with no positive or genuine response to his invitations.

Oh! that God would make you thirsty for salvation and thirsty for himself. You need to see the value of your soul and to realise that you are in danger of eternal ruin without

Christ. You need to feel as a real burden the weight of your unforgiven sin, and to acknowledge that it is against God, first and most important of all, that you have sinned. You need to have laid upon your conscience what it is to be guilty before God, to be unclean and separated from him, grieving him, under his just judgment. You need to see that the only one to whom you can turn for help and relief, the only one who can bring you any remedy and hope, the only one who can reconcile you to God, is the Lord Jesus Christ. You need to understand that every day you live you are actually dying, and that as you are (without the Lord Jesus Christ as your Saviour) you are totally unprepared to meet God, totally unfit to stand before him, totally unready to give an account of your life to him. You need to be brought to turn from your sin (in repentance) and to trust in Christ (in faith); or, as the apostle Paul puts it in a clear and concise manner: 'repentance towards God and faith towards our Lord Jesus Christ' (Acts 20:21).

Do you wonder sometimes why we make so much (or, better, why the Bible makes so much) of Christ? If you think back to a much earlier chapter of this book, you will remember how in Revelation 7:13-14 the Lord Jesus Christ is set forth as the only way to heaven. It is because he came, he lived, he died, he was buried, he rose again, he ascended into heaven again as the one (the only one, the unique one, the exclusive one) whom God the Father has appointed and provided to save sinners, to rescue sinners, to deliver sinners from sin and death and hell, and to take them safely and eternally to heaven. Now might be a suitable moment to look back to that chapter on the way to heaven and to remind yourself of what was opened up there concerning Christ.

How you need to recognise his voice when he speaks to

you, and not refuse him. He gives 'the water of life freely' (even his very self) to thirsty sinners who come to him for relief. It is his work, his office, and (what is more) his pleasure to receive sinners, and to give them pardon, life, peace and heaven. But his invitation will not be given for ever. One of these days it will be issued for the last time. Who knows when that will be? You do not, and neither do I. Can you still go on saying calmly to yourself, 'there is nothing here for me, this is no use to me, there is nothing that I need to hear or heed'? How long will you go on singing the same old lines, 'I'm not thirsty, I have no desire for Christ, don't keep bothering me with the water of life'? Are you going to keep on insisting that you want to be left alone?

Let me tell you solemnly that your words will ring in your ears, they will continue to haunt you, and one day they will rise up against you and condemn you for ever. Right now the Lord Jesus Christ holds open house for thirsty souls. There are no bouncers at his door to turn you away, handle you roughly or keep you from coming to him, for he himself promises that 'all that the Father gives me will come to me, and the one who comes to me I will by no means cast out' (John 6:37). He himself declares: 'If anyone thirsts, let him come to me and drink. He who believes in me, as the Scripture has said, out of his heart will flow rivers of living water' (John 7:37-38).

Look again at the lavishness of the invitation in Revelation 22:17. The thirsting one – let him come. The wishing one – let him take the water of life freely.

John Bunyan on the invitation to heaven
John Bunyan (1628-88) is one of the better known characters of church history, even among some who have no interest in

the gospel of the Lord Jesus Christ which he preached. Born in a cottage in the village of Elstow in Bedfordshire, he was the son of a poor tinker and spent his childhood mending pots and pans. This was to become his own trade in due time. He spent some days soldiering in the 1640s during the years of the Civil War. He has recorded God's dealings with him in his spiritual autobiography, *Grace Abounding to the Chief of Sinners*, and this has proved one of the most moving and enduring of his written works. No doubt, along with this volume, *Pilgrim's Progress* and *The Holy War* are the best known of his writings, though it is worth noting that his complete works run to three very full and exceedingly profitable volumes. He was imprisoned twice in Bedford jail during days when many non-conformist Christians were harassed in attempts to prevent them from gathering for worship and preaching.

The distinguished theologian John Owen was once asked by the king of England how a learned man like him could go 'to hear a tinker prate'; to which Owen replied, 'May it please your majesty, could I possess the tinker's abilities for preaching, I would willingly relinquish all my learning.'

One of John Bunyan's lesser known writings (found in the first volume of his works) bears the choice title *Come and Welcome to Jesus Christ*, having the following sub-title: or, a plain and profitable discourse on John 6:37, showing the cause, truth and manner of the coming of a sinner to Jesus Christ; with his happy reception and blessed entertainment. It is from this that I have selected the following portions.

In a section dealing with what it is that prevents a sinner from coming to Christ, he includes this. 'Coming sinner, Christ inviteth thee to dine and sup with him. He inviteth thee to a banquet of wine, yea, to come into his wine-cellar, and his banner over thee shall be love. But I doubt it, says the sinner: but, it is answered, he calls thee, invites thee to his banquet, flagons, apples; to his wine, and to the juice of his pomegranate. 'O, I fear, I doubt, I mistrust, I tremble in expectation of the contrary!' Come out of the man, thou dastardly ignorance! Be not afraid, sinner, only believe; 'He that cometh to Christ he will in no wise cast out.'

'Let the coming sinner, therefore, seek after more of the good knowledge of Jesus Christ. Press after it, seek it as silver, and dig for it as for hid treasure. This will embolden thee; this will make thee wax stronger and stronger. "I know whom I have believed", I know him, said Paul; and what follows? Why, "and I am persuaded that he is able to keep that which I have committed unto him, against that day." What had Paul committed to Jesus Christ? The answer is, He had committed to him his soul. But why did he commit his soul to him? Why, because he knew him. He knew him to be faithful, to be kind. He knew he would not fail him, nor forsake him; and therefore he laid his soul down at his feet, and committed it to him, to keep against that day'.

A little later, Bunyan presses the point that 'Christ would have comers not once think that he will cast them out', in the course of which we find this. 'Sinner, coming sinner, art thou for coming to Jesus Christ? Yes, says the sinner. Forsake thy wicked ways then. So I do, says the sinner. Why comest thou then so slowly? Because I am hindered. What hinders? Has God forbidden thee? No. Art thou not willing to come faster? Yes, yet I cannot. Well ... be plain with me, and tell me the reason and ground of thy discouragement. Why, says the sinner, though God forbids me not, and though I am willing to come faster, yet there naturally ariseth this, and that, and the other thought in my heart, and that hinders my speed to Jesus Christ. Sometimes I think I am not chosen; sometimes I think I am not called; sometimes I think I am come too late; and sometimes I think I know not what it is to come. Also one while I think I have no grace; and then again, that I cannot pray; and then again, I think that I am a very hypocrite. And these things keep me from coming to Jesus Christ.

'Look ye now, did not I tell you so? There are thoughts yet remaining in the heart, even of those who have forsaken their wicked ways; and with those thoughts they are more plagued than with anything else; because they hinder their coming to Jesus Christ; for the sin of unbelief, which is the original of all these thoughts, is that which besets a coming sinner more easily, than doth his ways. But, now, since Jesus Christ commands thee to forsake these thoughts, forsake them, coming sinner; and if thou forsake them not, thou transgressest the commands of Christ, and abidest thine own tormentor, and keepest thyself from establishment in grace. "If ye will not believe, surely ye shall not be established". Thus you see how Jesus Christ setteth himself against such thoughts, that any way discourage the coming sinner; and thereby truly vindicates the doctrine we have in hand ... that Jesus Christ would not have them, that in truth are coming to him, once think that he will cast them out.'

Finally, consider these words from Bunyan in answer to the question he puts as to the terms upon which a poor and needy sinner may have life in Jesus Christ. 'Answer: Freely. Sinner, dost thou hear. Thou mayest have it freely. Let him take the water of life freely. I will give him of the fountain of the water of life freely. "And when they had nothing to pay, he frankly forgave them both". Freely, without money, or without price ... Sinner, art thou thirsty? art thou weary? art thou willing? Come, then, and regard not your stuff; for all the good that is in Christ is offered to the coming sinner, without money and without price. He has life to give away to such as want it, and that hath not a penny to purchase it; and he will give it freely. Oh what a blessed condition is the coming sinner in!'

11

THE ALTERNATIVE TO HEAVEN

In the course of our consideration so far of heavenly things in the book of Revelation, we have been able to dwell upon some very choice, heartwarming and uplifting matters – such as heaven being God's dwelling place and filled with his praise, the purity and bliss of life there, the glorious promises given to every child of God with respect to heaven, the beatific vision, and so on. A full and faithful treatment of the subject, however, true to the whole counsel of God, cannot be content only with that, lest an imbalance be left, and room be given for all to imagine that it is well between their souls and God, and that heaven with all its glories is automatically for everyone. It is not.

There is life and there is death. Yet that is as far as many people's thinking ever goes. Or if their thinking sometimes goes further, their planning and preparations do not. Yet after life and death there is something else: eternity. And eternity spent in one of two places: there is eternity in heaven and there is eternity in hell. Right now, even at this very moment as you read these lines, you are on a journey to one or the other of them. The Lord Jesus Christ's parable of the rich man and Lazarus (Luke 16:19-31) makes this absolutely plain. If you are in any doubt about that (or even if you are not), take a moment now to read that parable through, asking the Holy Spirit to impress its truth upon your mind and heart and conscience.

So we must come now to consider this very solemn matter of the alternative to heaven. Notice the definite article: *the*

tive to heaven. It is not a case of alternative*s*. There is only one alternative to heaven, and that is hell. A verse in Revelation which focuses things clearly for us is 20:15, which arises in a section of the book which is concerned with the last judgment. 'And anyone not found written in the book of life was cast into the lake of fire.'

The reality of hell

The words stare at us from this verse: 'cast (or thrown) into the lake of fire'. The previous verse tells us something about 'the lake of fire': 'This is the second death.' The first death is death itself, ordinarily understood. The second death is the final judgment and the casting of the wicked into hell. 'The lake of fire' is just one of various names in the Bible for hell, each of which individually and all of which together leave us in no doubt over the fact that hell is real.

Mind you, had we lived in an earlier age we would hardly have had to spend time on this aspect, let alone emphasise it and underscore it. Hell's reality was a 'given'. It was accepted, understood and believed. No question was raised about it. Folk lived in the light of these twin truths: a real heaven and a real hell. Christians were sure of it. They testified to this in their life, preaching, conversation and doctrinal bases. Even those who were not Christians believed in hell. But these days that we now live in are very different. Both heaven and hell are doubted by men and women as a whole, and (most wretched of all) doubt is cast upon both of them (and especially hell) by those who reckon to be Christians, and even Christian leaders and Christian preachers, in the church of God.[31]

The fact is, though (and I declare this not as my own idea or upon my own authority, as if that would be any use, but from God's Word itself), that however unpalatable, unpleasing, unattractive, unacceptable, or unsavoury any-one may find this doctrine to be: hell is real, just as heaven is real. And real people are already there, including some we have known already in our lives. And real people will yet go there, including, it may be, some who are reading this book. It is striking that no one in the Bible has more to say upon the subject of hell than the Lord Jesus Christ him-self.

The awfulness of hell

Having insisted that hell is real, it is, in its very nature, awful, terrible and appalling. In all seriousness there is a sense in which we are 'lost for words' when it comes to speaking about hell or trying to describe it. It is *the* place to be fled from at all costs.

Look first at the name it is given in 20:15, the verse we are focussing upon: 'the lake of fire'. Imagine a lake of unfathomable depth. Down, down, down you go as you are hurled into it. There is no place to put your feet, no resting place, no solid ground. And then, 'of fire': a burning lake. Have you seen sometimes those pictures on television news reports, perhaps after a major oil spillage or explosion and consequent fire, when the very sea is on fire, so that men are falling not only into the water but into the fiery water, the burning water? It is the most awful scene of pain, agony and woe.

Yet, as already mentioned, 'the lake of fire' is only one of the Bible names for hell and pictures of hell.

Fire itself (with or without 'the lake') occurs frequently in both testaments. Here are some examples.

'Upon the wicked will he rain coals, fire and brimstone

and a burning wind; this shall be the portion of their cup'
(Ps. 11:6).

'The sinners in Zion are afraid; fearfulness has seized
the hypocrites: "Who among us shall dwell with the de-
vouring fire? Who among us shall dwell with everlasting
burnings?"' (Isa. 33:14).

'Who can stand before his indignation? And who can
endure the fierceness of his anger? His fury is poured out
like fire, and the rocks are thrown down by him' (Nahum
1:6).

John the Baptist, speaking of the Lord Jesus Christ, says:
'His winnowing fan is in his hand, and he will thoroughly
purge his threshing-floor, and gather his wheat into the barn;
but he will burn up the chaff with unquenchable fire' (Matt.
3:12).

'The Son of Man will send out his angels, and they will
gather out of his kingdom all things that offend, and those
who practise lawlessness, and will cast them into the furnace of fire. There will be wailing and gnashing of teeth'
(Matt. 13:41-42).

'Then he will also say to those on his left hand, "Depart
from me, you cursed, into the everlasting fire prepared for
the devil and his angels"' (Matt. 25:41).

Then there is the picture of the *worm* constantly gnawing
and eating away at those who are in hell. What a terrible
picture that gives of the everlasting torment, reproaches,
and accusations of conscience giving him no rest and peace
that the sinner in hell will experience. The Saviour's own
words in Mark 9:43-44 are the classic expression of this,
and combine with the Scripture teaching just reviewed on
fire: '... to go to hell, into the fire that shall never be quenched,
where "their worm does not die and the fire is not quenched".'

Then there is *Gehenna*. Spoken of in different Scriptures and consistently translated 'hell' in our English versions, this word underscores even more vividly the awful reality of eternal punishment. Gehenna was a place located south of Jerusalem and was the city's permanent rubbish dump. You could always see this smouldering sight. It was an utter wasteland, a vile place of desolation and hopelessness, without a single shred of cheer or brightness. This is the place spoken of in the verses already quoted, where 'their worm does not die and the fire is not quenched'.

It is the Lord Jesus Christ himself who speaks of Gehenna more than anyone else – indeed, on no less than eleven of the twelve occurrences of the word. Just consider these examples as indications of the serious and terrible nature of what he says:

'But whoever says, "You fool!" shall be in danger of hell fire' (Matt. 5:22)

'Serpents, brood of vipers! How can you escape the condemnation of hell?' (Matt. 23:33)

'And these will go away into everlasting punishment' (Matt. 25:46)

'And I say to you, my friends, do not be afraid of those who kill the body, and after that have no more that they can do. But I will show you whom you should fear: Fear him who, after he has killed, has power to cast into hell; yes, I say to you, fear him!' (Luke 12:4-5).

There are the references to '*outer darkness*' with weeping, wailing and gnashing of teeth. Feel the full force of them:

'But the sons of the kingdom will be cast into outer darkness. There will be weeping and gnashing of teeth' (Matt. 8:12).

'Then the king said to the servants, "Bind him hand and foot, take him away, and cast him into outer darkness; there will be weeping and gnashing of teeth"' (Matt. 22:13).

What pictures of utter despair, blackness and gloom, though notice again that they arise in the course of the Lord Jesus Christ's own teaching. The scene is a desperate one: no day ever dawns, no morning ever comes, no sun ever shines, no clear sky ever appears, it is never day but always night.

To add to all of this, Revelation uses two other significant words. There is *the prison* (in connection with Satan being let loose, 20:7), with its picture of slavery and bondage, and the very inhabitants in fear and hatred of one another. No fond 'camaraderie' there. And there is *the bottomless pit* (mentioned in 9:1-2). What thoughts of darkness, ruin, abandonment and hopelessness that conjures up. While these two descriptions (the prison and the pit) apply particularly to the present abode of the devil and his legions of fallen angels (William Hendriksen comments, for example, 'the abyss indicates hell before the final judgment'), they remind us of what a terrible state it will be for those who, with the devil, are consigned to hell. They add sombrely to the total picture.

But the sting in the tail of hell's awfulness is still to be mentioned. It is this. All that Scripture says of the awfulness of hell is not only true, but true *eternally*. For ever! The lake of fire goes on burning. The hungry worm goes on feeding. The rubbish dump goes on rotting and smouldering. The darkness goes on spreading its cloak of gloom. The wailing and the crying is always heard. To be condemned to hell is truly to be condemned for ever.

Because of the horror of this, people have tried to get

around it with ideas of their own; but they are only ideas of their own. One person's ideas are as wrong as another's once we are left to our own ideas. So you get, for example, *purgatory* (a place to go after death in order to be refined and prepared for heaven in one way and another); *conditional immortality* (which argues that while man ordinarily is mortal, God will grant him immortality upon his repentance and faith: everyone else will be annihilated or extinguished); *annihilationism* itself (which, appearing in various forms, claims either that everyone or that just the wicked will disappear to 'nothingness', thus reducing hell to 'non-existence' or 'non-reality'); and *re-incarnation* (having a cycle of lives, and re-appearing at different times and in different personas). It will be seen straightaway, however, that all of these suggestions (and others besides) have one fundamental thing in common: a refusal to accept the teaching of the Bible, the Word of God, and a determined insistence to mark out some other way instead. Consequently, they all fall to pieces. The straight-talking statement of Proverbs 14:12 is apposite here: 'There is a way which seems right to a man, but its end is the way of death.'

The justice of hell

A word is necessary upon this. Imagine a conversation along these classic and common lines. Someone may well look at a verse like Revelation 20:15 (or, look on to what is said in 21:8, 'But the cowardly, unbelieving, abominable, murderers, sexually immoral, sorcerers, idolaters, and all liars shall have their part in the lake which burns with fire and brimstone, which is the second death'), and say: 'Hold on there! Wait a moment! Not so fast!'

So you say to them, 'Why? What's the problem?' To which

they respond, 'It's not fair'. 'What's not fair?,' you ask. 'The whole thing isn't fair', they say, 'the whole business of hell just isn't fair'. (In passing, you'll notice that folk don't tend to complain that heaven isn't fair, but the charge is often brought that hell is unfair).

It is very important to understand that any attack upon the justice and fairness of hell is an attack upon the justice and fairness of God, who has decreed all matters of heaven and hell. Hence the well-known form the attack often takes: how can a God of love send people to hell? But, as well as observing in response that while God is most certainly a God of love, he is not *only* a God of love, bear in mind also Romans 9:20: 'But indeed, O man, who are you to reply against God?' The NIV has 'to talk back to God'. The point, in brief, is this. If you are to have right thoughts concerning the justice of hell, you must begin by having right thoughts concerning God and the justice of God.

Paul Helm has stated the matter exactly. 'If God is supremely just, and just in a sense which is recognisable as just by his human creatures, and if hell exists, exists because it is ordained by God, then hell must be just.' And again: 'So hell is a place of justice, where punishment is dispensed not in accordance with the warped and partial and ignorant procedures of human society, but immaculately, in accordance with the standards of him who is supremely just. There will be no cause for complaint. Every mouth will be stopped, not forcibly but by the recognition of the justice of the proceedings.'[33]

The verse of Revelation we have been focussing upon (20:15) comes from a section which is concerned with the last judgment. Central to this portion of Scripture is the vivid statement of verse 11: 'Then I saw a great white throne and him who sat upon it, from whose face the earth and the heaven fled away. And there was found no place for them.' Notice how it sets forth the *sovereignty* of God (seated on a throne); the *mightiness* of God (it is a great throne); and the *holiness and purity* of God (it is 'a great white throne'). As the same verse and the following verses continue, there is also the *wrath and terror* of God (as earth and heaven flee from his presence, v11b); the *inescapableness* of God (brought out in v. 12a and 13); and the *absolute justice* of God (the principles of strictest justice, God knowing precisely what is 'in' a man, v. 12b). We are all laid bare before him to whom we must give an account and with whom we all have to do.

Would you object to hell being hell? You cannot – unless you object to God being God. Even those whose punishment hell will be will recognise the justice of their plight, for their knees as well will bow 'at the name of Jesus', and their tongues too will 'confess that Jesus Christ is Lord, to the glory of God the Father' (Phil. 2:10-11). That must be so, since those verses speaks of 'every knee' and 'every tongue' – though in the case of impenitent sinners, of course, this bowing and confessing will not be out of any adoration of or love for God, but because God is God and is seen and acknowledged by all creation to be God.

The escape from hell
This is surely the note upon which we need to end this section of our study. Have you ever wondered why there is so much teaching in the Bible on hell, and why the teaching of the Lord Jesus Christ recorded in the Gospels is so full of it? The answer is this: to warn us of hell that we might flee from it. Hell is not in the Bible for us to debate it or to reject

it. It is there so that we might escape from it! Hence the urgency of needing to 'flee from the wrath to come' (Matt. 3:7).

Let us take a moment for another reminder of the position. God is all glorious. He is full of majesty, holy through and through. He alone is to be worshipped, his laws are to be obeyed, his way is to be followed – by all of us.

But we are sinners – all of us. We are sinners by nature (in our minds and hearts) and sinners by practice (in our words and deeds). Left to ourselves we do not worship God, stand in awe of him or give him the glory. We do not keep his commandments. We do not walk in his ways. We are 'by nature children of wrath' (Eph. 2:3).

So what is the holy God who hates sin to do? He must punish us with death. He must condemn us to hell. He has said, 'the soul who sins shall die' (Ezek. 18:4), and that means not only dying the first death (death at the end of our life) but dying the second death (the lake of fire).

Is that it, then? Is there no hope for sinners? Are we all alike doomed? Since God is angry with the wicked every day, are we all done for? 'It is a fearful thing to fall into the hands of the living God' (Heb. 10:31).

But if we are to 'flee from the wrath to come', where are we to run to? What is the way of escape? Where is the place of safety? The answer, of course, takes us to the very heart of the gospel once again, for it directs us to 'Jesus who delivers us from the wrath to come' (1 Thess. 1:10). He, God's Son from heaven, is himself the glorious door of mercy, the matchless way of salvation, the provided way of escape. Indeed, is not God's way of escape mentioned even in our focus text? Look again at Revelation 20:15, at the end of the verse, and the mention there (not for the first time in our studies) of 'the book of life'. That, you remember, is God's secret book, written before the creation of the world, in which are written all the names of all those whom it will be the sovereign pleasure of the God of all grace to save from their sins, reconcile to himself, and bring safely to heaven.

Your response to this news, as we considered in an earlier chapter, is not to start philosophising or speculating upon whether or not your name is in that book, for you cannot take it down from the shelf to see. The question for you is: where is your sin? Is it still on you: are you still in your sin and pressing on with your sin? Or is your sin laid upon the sinless one: are you looking to Jesus, who, by his perfect and obedient life, his sin-bearing death upon the cross, and his glorious resurrection from the dead, can deliver you from the coming wrath? Your sins left upon you will take you to hell. You will be thrown into the lake of fire. But your sins laid on Jesus – ah! then he will take you to heaven. Are you clear on that?

> He bears our sins upon the tree;
> He brings us mercy from above.
>
> Thomas Kelly

Thomas Boston on the alternative to heaven

Thomas Boston (1676-1732) was born in Duns (Berwickshire) and is best remembered as the minister of Ettrick, a town in the Scottish borders, where he laboured in the gospel for twenty-five years, with, eventually, much spiritual blessing.

His life and ministry were marked by both joys and sorrows. His wife, Catherine, whom he described as 'a woman of great worth, whom I therefore passionately loved, and inwardly honoured', was subject to great affliction. He gave himself unstintingly to the work of God, and was greatly exercised for the people in his spiritual charge.

Many writings flowed from his pen, including *A View of the Covenant of Grace*, *The Crook in the Lot* (sermons on Ecclesiastes 7:13, sub-titled The Sovereignty and Wisdom of God in the Afflictions of Men Displayed), *A Soliloquy on The Art of Man-Fishing* (a treatment of Christ's words in Matthew 4:19 presenting 'a pattern to every preacher of the gospel', and described by one admirer as a 'little gem of Scottish piety'), and his *Memoirs*. However, it may be argued that his most significant and enduring volume is the one entitled *Human Nature in its Fourfold State*. John Macleod says of it, 'a better handbook of sound theology one can hardly find than what is supplied by this master-piece'. The 'fourfold state' in view is that 'of primitive integrity, entire depravity, begun recovery and consummate happiness or misery' (that is to say, 'the biblical teaching on the four different 'states' of man's relationship with God – innocence, sin, grace and glory').[34]

On the very opening page of his treatment of hell, Boston makes this memorable statement: 'in the other world there is a prison for the wicked, as well as a palace for saints.' Just a few lines later he writes these words. 'The last thing which our Lord did, before he left the earth, was, "He lifted up his hands, and blessed his disciples" (Luke 24:50-51). But the last thing he will do, before he leaves the throne, is to curse and condemn his enemies.'

Ponder carefully the following extracts from Boston's famous work, beginning with this on the aggravations of the torments of the wicked in hell. He mentions three. The first is this: 'They are ready for them, for they are not to expect a moment's respite. The fire is prepared and ready to catch hold of those who are thrown into it.' And the second: 'They will have the society of the devils in their torments, being shut up with them in hell. They must depart into the same fire, prepared for Beelzebub, the prince of devils, and his angels; namely, other reprobate angels who fell with him, and became devils. It is said to be prepared for them; because they sinned and were condemned to hell before man sinned. This speaks further terror to the damned, that they must go into the same torments, and place of torment, with the devil and his angels. They hearkened to his temptations, and they must partake in his torments: his works they would do, and they must receive the wages, which is death. In this life they joined with devils in enmity against God and Christ, and the way of holiness; and in the other, they must lodge with them.' And the third: 'The last aggravation of their torment is the eternal duration thereof; they must depart into everlasting fire. This is what puts a top-stone on their misery, namely, that it shall never have an end.'

Hear him upon the curse under which the damned shall be shut up. 'As to the curse under which the damned shall be shut up in hell, it is the terrible sentence of the law, by which they are bound over to the wrath of God as transgressors. This curse does not first seize them when standing before the tribunal to receive their sentence; but they were born under it, they led their lives under it in this world, they died under it, rose with it out of their graves; and the Judge finding it upon them, sends them away with it into the pit, where it shall lie on them through all the ages of eternity. By nature all men are under the curse; but it is removed from the elect by virtue of their union with Christ. It abides on the rest of sinful mankind, and by it they are devoted to destruction ... separate and set apart from the rest of mankind, unto evil, as vessels of wrath; set up as marks for the arrows of divine wrath; and made the common receptacle and shore of vengeance.'

Boston speaks in a most moving manner of the misery of the damned – 'a misery which the tongues of men and angels cannot sufficiently express.' 'God always acts like himself,' he observes; 'no favours can be compared to his, and his wrath and terrors are without parallel. As the saints in heaven are advanced to the highest pitch of happiness, so the damned in hell arrive at the height of misery.'

He describes the punishment of those in hell in a twofold sense: the punishment of loss and the punishment of sense. On the punishment of loss, consider this. 'The punishment of loss which the damned shall undergo, is separation from the Lord ... This will be a stone upon their grave's mouth ... that will hold them down for ever. They shall be eternally separated from God and Christ. Christ is the way to the Father: but the way, as to them, shall be everlastingly blocked up, the bridge shall be drawn, and the great gulf fixed; so shall they be shut up in a state of eternal separation from God the Father, Son, and Holy Ghost ... They cannot be locally separated from God, they cannot be in a place where he is not; since he is, and will be present everywhere: "If I make my bed in hell", says the psalmist, "behold thou art there" (Ps. 139:8). But they shall be miserable beyond expression, in a relative separation from God. Though he will be present in the very centre of their souls, if I may so express it, while they are wrapped up in fiery flames, in utter darkness, it shall only be to feed them with the vinegar of his wrath, and to punish them with the emanations of his revenging justice: they shall never more taste of his goodness and bounty, nor have the least glimpse of hope from him.

They will see His heart to be absolutely alienated from them, and that it cannot be towards them; that they are the party against whom the Lord will have indignation for ever. They shall be deprived of the glorious presence and enjoyment of God: they shall have no part in the beatific vision; nor see anything in God towards them, but one wave of wrath rolling after another. This will bring upon them overwhelming floods of sorrow for evermore. They shall never taste the rivers of pleasures which the saints in heaven enjoy; but shall have an everlasting winter and a perpetual night, because the Sun of Righteousness has departed from them, and so they are left in utter darkness. So great as heaven's happiness is, so great will their loss be: for they can have none of it for ever.'

Ever the lover of souls, Boston closes in this fashion. 'And now, if you would be saved from the wrath to come, and never go into this place of torment, take no rest in your natural state; believe the sinfulness and misery of it, and labour to get out of it quickly, fleeing unto Jesus Christ by faith. Sin in you is the seed of hell; and if the guilt and reigning power of it be not removed in time, they will bring you to the second death in eternity. There is no way to get them removed, but by receiving Christ as He is offered in the Gospel, for justification and sanctification: and He is now offered to you with all His salvation ... Jesus Christ is the Mediator of peace, and the fountain of holiness: He it is who delivers us from the wrath to come ... And the terrors of hell, as well as the joys of heaven, are set before you, to stir you up to a cordial receiving of Him, with all His salvation; and to incline you to the way of holiness, in which alone you can escape the everlasting fire. May the Lord Himself make them effectual to that end!'

12

THE FOCUS OF HEAVEN

As we prepare to take our leave of this study of the doctrine of heaven in the book of Revelation, the book with which the word of God closes, one very appropriate matter remains upon which to finish. What is the special focus of heaven? Or, rather, who is that special focus? The answer is given very clearly in 5:6, and is found to be the Lord Jesus Christ. Surely this will not surprise us! Here is the verse: 'And I looked, and behold, in the midst of the throne and of the four living creatures, and in the midst of the elders, stood a Lamb as though it had been slain, having seven horns and seven eyes, which are the seven spirits of God sent out into all the earth.'

Many names and titles are given in the Scriptures to the Lord Jesus Christ. It is a most profitable and thrilling study to trace them right the way through. He is, for example, the Son of God and the Son of Man; King of kings and Lord of lords; Wonderful Counsellor, Mighty God, Everlasting Father, Prince of Peace; Immanuel, meaning God with us; Commander of the army of the LORD; the Root and Offspring of David, the Bright and Morning Star; the hope of glory; the Sun of Righteousness; the bread of life, the light of the world, the door of the sheep, the good shepherd, the resurrection and the life, the way, the truth and the life, and the true vine; the power of God and the wisdom of God; the rose of Sharon, the lily of the valleys, an apple tree among the trees of the woods, chief among ten thousand, altogether lovely – and so the list goes on, because the whole of the Bible, from beginning to end, testifies of him (compare John 5:39). No doubt you can add to this list for yourself.[35]

But there is one name in particular which stands out (and certainly, as we have discovered, which stands out in Revelation). It stands out because it is especially suitable for him, and it stands out because it is especially precious to us who belong to him. That name is the Lamb. And this is the name of the Lord Jesus Christ which is before us now, and in which he appears as the focus of heaven.

In this fifth chapter of Revelation, the apostle John, you remember, is looking into heaven. He is 'in the Spirit'. He has been given what we might call a 'spiritual ascent' into heaven, a view through heaven's open door. What did he see? Hear his own testimony: 'And I looked, and behold ... a Lamb.' John saw the risen, ascended, glorified Lord Jesus Christ, the second Person of the Trinity, with a human nature which he still bears in heaven and ever will bear. The Lord Jesus Christ is himself the focus of heaven, the focal point of heaven. But what may we say of him as such, from this verse, 5:6?

He is the Lamb slain

John is very specific in his statement of what he saw: 'a Lamb as though it had been slain'. Not merely did he see a Lamb, but a slain Lamb, a sacrificial Lamb. It was a Lamb which, while it was now alive (very much so) had once been dead.

Recall the words of the Lord Jesus earlier in the book: 'I am he who lives, and was dead, and behold, I am alive for evermore' (1:18). He is 'a Lamb as though it had been slain'. Jesus is 'the Lamb of God who takes away the sin of the

world' (John 1:29). He is the sin-bearing Lamb. The Lord
Jesus Christ, there in heaven, is seen in all the glory, all the
beauty, all the majesty and all the uniqueness of his saving
work. Christ Jesus and him crucified; risen, yes!, glorified,
yes!: but first, crucified, and crucified even for us, his
people.

He is the one of whom the prophet Isaiah spoke in that
matchless passage in his 53rd chapter, on substitution.
Meditate upon those words again. 'Surely he has borne our
griefs and carried our sorrows; yet we esteemed him
stricken, smitten by God, and afflicted. But he was wounded
for our transgressions, he was bruised for our iniquities;
the chastisement for our peace was upon him, and by his
stripes we are healed. All we like sheep have gone astray;
we have turned, every one, to his own way; and the LORD
has laid on him the iniquity of us all' (53:4-6).

The Lord Jesus is not now upon the cross, for he is in
heaven itself; but 'Christ crucified' is a very precious and
poignant way for the believer of meditating upon him. It
reminds us of his sufferings and death in our place. It makes
us think of what that solemn verse means: 'He who did not
spare his own Son, but delivered him up for us all, how
shall he not with him also freely give us all things?' (Rom.
8:32). It recalls to us the appalling cost of our salvation
(free to us, but costly – oh! so costly – to God). When we
were brought to faith in Christ, it was to 'the Lamb slain'
that we looked. As we press on through our Christian lives,
still it is to 'the Lamb slain' that we look. And when we are
landed safely in glory's bliss, then too it will be to 'the Lamb
slain' that we shall forever look.

It was as 'the Lamb slain from the foundation of the
world' (Rev. 13:8) that the Lord Jesus Christ agreed to

become our sacrifice and our Saviour. It was as 'the Lamb slain' that he loved us and proved his love for us at Calvary on the cruel cross. It is as 'the Lamb slain' that we love him, that we are taken up with him, that we boast and glory in him, and that he is precious to us, prized by us, and that we delight especially to declare his praise.

> All glory and praise
> To the Lamb that was slain,
> Who has borne all our sins
> And has cleansed every stain.
>
> Hallelujah! Thine the glory,
> Hallelujah! we sing;
> Hallelujah! Thine the glory,
> Our praise now we bring.
>
> William P Mackay

It is as 'the Lamb slain' that we shall be presented to him – remember it is 'the marriage of the Lamb' (19:7). It is as 'the Lamb slain' that we shall be with him forever. He is to us (to use a Scripture phrase) 'a husband of blood' (Exod. 4:26). Behold here, all together, the love, wisdom, power, justice, holiness and mercy of God. It is 'the Lamb slain' who is the object of our faith, our admiration, our devotion, our confidence and our love. It is he who died. He is the Lamb that was slain.

> Here I rest, in wonder viewing
> All my sins on Jesus laid,
> And a full redemption flowing
> From the sacrifice He made
>
> W W Shirley

So we are not surprised to discover the apostle Paul testifying to the Corinthians, 'For I determined not to know

anything among you except Jesus Christ and him crucified'
(1 Cor. 2:2), or declaring to the Galatians, 'But God forbid
that I should glory except in the cross of our Lord Jesus
Christ, by which the world has been crucified to me, and I
to the world' (Gal. 6:14).

So, to quote Spurgeon, from a sermon on Revelation
5:6, 'the teaching of the passage is that the Lord Jesus, in
his sacrificial character, is the most prominent object in the
heavenly world. So far from substitution being done with,
and laid aside as a temporary expedient, it remains the object of universal wonder and adoration'. It is as the Lamb
that the Lord Jesus 'is the centre of the wonderful circle
which makes up the fellowship of heaven'.[36]

He is the Lamb triumphant

The book of Revelation (as well we know) is a book of
pictures and symbols. Many of them are very strange, and
often one passes rapidly after another. In the verse
immediately before 5:6, the Lord Jesus Christ is referred to
by one of the elders with a description very different from
that of a lamb. He calls him a lion! 'Behold, the Lion of the
tribe of Judah ... has prevailed (NIV, triumphed).' So maybe
John then expected to see a lion; but he records that he saw
a lamb! Indeed, the word he uses for 'lamb' actually means
'a little lamb' – maybe to indicate the Lord Jesus' tenderness
to his people, his approachableness, his availability. But
the 'little lamb' is also a lion! He is great. He is glorious.
He is majestic. He is awesome. He is without compare.
And he is all of this very especially, John is discovering
here, in the outworking of the purposes of God.

We need to take a moment to explain the business here
concerning the scroll. In the opening verses of chapter 5

John records first what he saw and then what he heard: 'And I saw in the right hand of him who sat on the throne a scroll written inside and on the back, sealed with seven seals. Then I saw a strong angel proclaiming with a loud voice, "Who is worthy to open the scroll and to loose its seals?"' It turned out that there was no one who could do this: 'And no one in heaven or on the earth or under the earth was able to open the scroll, or to look at it.' This caused much grief to the apostle – at which point 'one of the elders' spoke to him with good news. There is one who can 'open the scroll and ... loose its seven seals'. Who is that? The Lion who is the Lamb! He is worthy, and he is able. He 'has prevailed'.

What is this all about? This scroll represents the whole of God's plan of history, all that he has purposed, all that he will bring to pass, including (not least) his great plan of salvation or scheme of redemption. The fact that the scroll is 'sealed with seven seals' indicates this wholeness, fulness, and completeness (such is the significance so often of the number 'seven' in the Bible), and that it is sealed at all indicates that God's plan is not only fixed but hidden, until he chooses to make it known. But how will he make it known? In whom will he reveal it and bring his pleasure to pass? The answer is, in and through his own Son, the Lord Jesus Christ. Consequently he is the only one who could 'open the scroll and ... loose its seven seals'. So we read: 'Then he came and took the scroll out of the right hand of him who sat on the throne' (5:7).

And how has the Lord Jesus Christ 'prevailed'? How has he 'triumphed'? Not by weapons of warfare, armies or the force of human argument, but in the most remarkable way: by his 'blood' (5:9). He 'made himself of no reputation, taking the form of a servant, and coming in the likeness of men. And being found in appearance as a man, he humbled himself and became obedient to the point of death, even the death of the cross' (Phil. 2:7-8). But that was no weakness! The one who is the Lamb is also the Lion. As the very Lamb who was slain, he is the Lion who has prevailed and triumphed – over sin and Satan, death and hell. 'For this purpose the Son of God was manifested, that he might destroy the works of the devil' (1 John 3:8). He has prevailed victoriously and has 'redeemed us to God' and 'made us kings and priests to God' (5:9-10). He has shown himself to be 'King of kings and Lord of lords' (19:16). Moreover, in consequence of his victories, 'God also has highly exalted him and given him the name which is above every name, that at the name of Jesus every knee should bow, of those in heaven, and of those on earth, and of those under the earth, and that every tongue should confess that Jesus Christ is Lord, to the glory of God the Father' (Phil. 2:9-11).

This is a magnificent theme – the triumphs of Christ – which runs through the whole of the Bible, Old and New Testament alike. It is affirmed prophetically in such Psalms as Psalm 2 (especially verses 6-9), Psalm 68 (note particularly verse 18, which is taken up in Ephesians 4:8), and – perhaps most exquisitely of all – Psalm 72, with its matchless closing verses which are so familiar in the metrical version:

> His name for ever shall endure;
> Last like the sun it shall:
> Men shall be bless'd in him, and bless'd
> All nations shall him call.
>
> Now blessed be the Lord our God,
> The God of Israel,

For he alone doth wondrous works,
In glory that excel.

And blessed be his glorious name
To all eternity:
The whole earth let his glory fill.
Amen, so let it be.

(Ps. 72:17-19, metrical version)

And it is expressed by the Lord Jesus Christ himself on such an occasion as his testimony in Matthew 28:18: 'All authority has been given to me in heaven and on earth.'

Do not be misled by the picture of the 'little lamb', or the talk exclusively of 'gentle Jesus, meek and mild'. Certainly there is none meeker and none milder, hence the reference in 2 Corinthians 10:1 to 'the meekness and gentleness of Christ' and his own precious words in Matthew 11:29, 'for I am gentle and lowly in heart'. But the Lamb is a Lion. He rules and he reigns. He sustains all things by his powerful word. While 'he who believes on him will by no means be put to shame', yet to others he will be 'a stone of stumbling and a rock of offence' (1 Pet. 2:6,8). His gospel is to some 'the fragrance of life' but to others 'the smell of death' (2 Cor. 2:16, NIV).

He is not to be trifled with, but trusted completely 'to bring us to God' (1 Pet. 3:18 – some versions translate 'you' rather than 'us'). He must not be taken for granted or regarded lightly. Remember the call of Psalm 2:12: 'Kiss the Son, lest he be angry, and you perish in the way, when his wrath is kindled but a little. Blessed are all those who put their trust in him.' 'The wrath of the Lamb' is, of course, a vital theme in the book of Revelation itself (6:16-17).

At the end of the first volume of his works, Jonathan

Edwards has a sermon on 5:6, which he entitles *The Excellency of Christ*. The use he makes of the text is to set forth the truth that 'There is an admirable conjunction of diverse excellencies in Jesus Christ'. He proceeds to say this: 'The lion and the lamb, though very diverse kinds of creatures, yet each have their peculiar excellencies. The lion excels in strength, and in the majesty of his appearance and voice: the lamb excels in meekness and patience, besides the excellent nature of the creature as good for food, and yielding that which is fit for our clothing, and being suitable to be offered in sacrifice to God. But we see that Christ is in the text compared to both; because the diverse excellencies of both wonderfully meet in him.'

The way he then develops this and applies it is most profitable and enlightening. As a taster, just consider these 'heads'. 'There do meet in Jesus Christ infinite highness and infinite condescension ... infinite justice and infinite grace ... infinite glory and lowest humility ... infinite majesty and transcendent meekness ... deepest reverence towards God and equality with God ... infinite worthiness of good and the greatest patience under sufferings of evil ... an exceeding spirit of obedience with supreme dominion over heaven and earth ... absolute sovereignty and perfect resignation .... self-sufficiency and an entire trust and reliance on God.' It all has the effect of conveying to us a strong reminder, when considering the Person of the Lord Jesus Christ, never to divide what God has joined together.

Behold, then, the glory of the Saviour of sinners, who promises, 'All that the Father gives me will come to me, and the one who comes to me I will by no means cast out' (John 6:37) – the words of the Lamb who was slain. But lest any still think that they can do as they please with his invitations and promises of grace, 'Behold, the Lion of the tribe of Judah', triumphant, regal, glorious, sovereign, eternal, who, if he does not say to you, 'Come, you blessed of my Father, inherit the kingdom prepared for you from the foundation of the world', will say to you, 'Depart from me, you cursed, into the everlasting fire prepared for the devil and his angels' (Matt. 25:34,41).

He is the Lamb adored

What should be our response, and the response of the entire creation, to this Lord Jesus Christ? He is *the Lion* who has prevailed and triumphed, the conquering one, the one who declares God to man, the one through whom God brings his purposes and promises to pass, the only one who is worthy and able to open the scroll. He is *the Lamb* who has been slain and has redeemed us to God by his blood. Moreover, the symbolic reference to him 'having seven horns and seven eyes, which are the seven spirits of God sent out into all the earth', add very much to the total picture, and speak of his omnipotence and his omniscience, and how, after his death and resurrection he sent his Holy Spirit from heaven. What should be our response to him?

We need to be guided and directed by the response recorded here in Revelation 5 itself, for we can be sure it is the correct one: worship, adoration and praise. The fact is that the Lord Jesus Christ who is the focus of heaven is the Lamb adored! As Spurgeon puts it, in the same sermon quoted from earlier: 'He dwelleth as a King in his central pavilion, and this is the joy of the host, that the King is in the midst of them.' And this fifth chapter, from verse 8 to the end, demonstrates this most memorably and magnificently in no less than three distinct outbursts of adoration and praise.

First off, in verses 8-10, are 'the four living creatures and the twenty-four elders' (the former very likely being cherubim, the highest order of angels, and the latter certainly being symbolic of the whole church of God). Notice that they 'fell down before the Lamb' (another plain indication of the deity of Christ, for God alone is to be worshipped and adored), and that 'they sang a new song'. The Bible contains many calls to us to 'sing a new song to the Lord' (a classic example is Isaiah 42:10). There is a vital sense in which the praise of God, and so of the Lamb, is ever new, and will continuue so throughout eternity in the new heaven and new earth where nothing will ever become stale or old. How appropriate it is, moreover, that the new song should be sung by new creatures, the redeemed of the Lord. We are reminded of another verse from Isaiah, a verse very much looking heavenwards: 'And the ransomed of the LORD shall return, and come to Zion with singing, with everlasting joy on their heads. They shall obtain joy and gladness, and sorrow and sighing shall flee away' (35:10, and also 51:11).

Then, secondly, in verses 11-12, comes 'the voice of many angels around the throne, the living creatures, and the elders' all together. And what a company they comprise: 'and the number of them was ten thousand times ten thousand, and thousands of thousands'. Their praise formed a sevenfold ascription of adoring glory acknowledging the worthiness of the Lamb: his divine power, inexhaustible riches, infinite wisdom, matchless strength, supreme honour, eternal glory and ceaseless blessing. The definite article appears at the head of this sequence, before the mention of Christ's power, and 'covers', as it were, the whole list, by way of a reminder of what is due to God alone, for he will not share his worship with another.

The third and concluding praise here, in verses 13-14, pictures all creation singing together – 'every creature which is in heaven and on the earth and under the earth and such as are in the sea, and all that are in them'. The adoration they ascribe to 'him who sits on the throne, and to the Lamb' is 'for ever and ever', which is (literally) 'unto the ages of the ages'! This is followed with a final, climactic 'Amen' from the four living creatures, and the twenty-four elders falling down and worshipping 'him who lives for ever and ever'.

> Salvation to God
>   Who sits on the throne!
> Let all cry aloud,
>   And honour the Son:
> The praises of Jesus
>   The angels proclaim,
> Fall down on their faces,
>   And worship the Lamb.
>
> Then let us adore,
>   And give Him His right,
> All glory and power,
>   All wisdom and might,
> All honour and blessing,
>   With angels above,
> And thanks never-ceasing,
>   And infinite love.
>
>   Charles Wesley

It needs to be affirmed that the Lord Jesus Christ can never be prized too highly or praised too much. It was John Newton who said this: 'It will not be a burden to me at the hour of death that I have thought too highly of Jesus, expected too much of Him myself or laboured too much in commending and setting Him forth to others.' How we wish that even now we could and would praise him as we ought. Never forget this: 'that to fall before the throne, to show humility, reverence for the Lamb, and also to adore Him – these things are an infallible mark and evidence of having an interest in Christ'.[37]

Here, then, is the focus of heaven: the Lamb slain, the Lamb triumphant, and the Lamb adored. Is it any wonder he is represented in 5:6 as 'in the midst of the throne'? Where else would he be, than with everyone else encircling him, revolving around him, looking to him and united in him.

With this in mind, I cannot forbear a word of application as we approach the close of our study. Would we know more and more of the life of heaven even while we continue for the time being here upon the earth? Then why do we seem to know (comparatively speaking) so little of it? Is there not a clue in what we have just been considering? Where do we so often go wrong as Christians and as churches in this matter? Without wishing to sound in any sense simplistic surely our problem so much of the time is this: we do not give to the Lamb his proper place. And what is that proper place? In the midst. In the centre. All looking to him. All delighting in him. All taken up with him. All seeking to be like him. All concerned to glorify him. All adoring him. In other words, the Lord Jesus Christ – the Lamb – is to be at the centre of the worship, at the centre of the preaching, at the centre of the prayer meetings, at the centre of our conversations and fellowship, at the centre of our individual lives, our marriages and our family lives, at the centre of our hearts. He who is the focus of heaven – and for ever will be – needs to be our focus continually, worthy of our purest worship, our supreme affection, our first love, our absolute devotion and our unquestioning obedience. Those things which would put him anywhere else but 'in the midst' or 'at the centre' must go, and the sooner they go the better: our coldness, worldliness, idleness, sinfulness, discontentedness, and all the rest of the sad and sorry list of things which so easily affect us all.

Let no one have our hearts but the Lord Jesus Christ! May the one who is the very heart and focus of heaven be all in all to us, to the glory of the entire Godhead. And may our hope, increasingly, while here on the earth, be this: to be with the Lamb, to see the Lamb, to know the Lamb, to serve the Lamb, to please the Lamb, to be like the Lamb, and then, in God's perfect time, to join with the whole company of heaven in the praise and worship and adoration of the Lamb.

John Owen on the focus of heaven

John Owen (1616-1683) was born near the city of Oxford. He had three brothers and a sister, and wrote on one occasion of his father (Henry Owen, a Puritan vicar) that he was 'a Nonconformist all his days, and a painful labourer in the vineyard of the Lord'.

Owen studied at Oxford University, and his varied ministry included periods at Fordham, near Colchester in Essex, and Coggeshall in the same county. When he was only thirty-two years old he was called upon to preach before Parliament on the day after the execution of Charles I in 1649, when he took as his text Jeremiah 15:19-20. He served as chaplain to Oliver Cromwell both in Ireland and Scotland. In 1651 he became Dean of Christ Church, Oxford, and, the following year, was appointed Vice-Chancellor of the University. In later life he ministered in London.

His writings are vast, volume upon volume, yet still in print today and read and treasured by many of the Lord's people. A choice record is preserved from the end of his life, which bears upon both his writings and heaven. On 24 August 1683, William Payne (who was a Puritan minister in Saffron Walden, and was attending to the business of seeing Owen's work *Meditations on the Glory of Christ* through to publication) called on him to inform him that the work was already being printed. Owen's moving reply was: 'I am glad to hear it; but O brother Payne! the long wished for day is come at last, in which I shall see that glory in another manner than I have ever done, or was capable of doing, in this world.' He died later that same day.

Our study closes with a quotation from the second volume of John Owen's works, which deals with communion with God.[38] In the course of this treatise Owen spends some time opening up the second part of chapter 5 of the Song of Songs, where the Lord Jesus Christ (the Bridegroom) is described in an exquisite and fulsome manner by the Christian/church (the bride), culminating in the statement concerning him, 'Yes, he is altogether lovely. This is my beloved, and this is my friend' (Song 5:16).

"When the spouse hath gone thus far in the description of him, she concludes all in this general assertion: 'He is wholly desirable – altogether to be desired or beloved'. As if she should have said – 'I have thus reckoned up some of the perfections of the creatures (things of most value, price, usefulness, beauty, glory, here below), and compared some of the excellencies of my Beloved unto them. In this way of allegory I can carry things no higher; I find nothing better or more desirable to shadow out and to present his loveliness and desirableness: but, alas! all this comes short of his perfections, beauty and comeliness; 'he is *all wholly* to be desired, to be beloved'.

Lovely in his *person* – in the glorious all-sufficiency of his Deity, gracious purity and holiness of his humanity, authority and majesty, love and power.

Lovely in his *birth* and incarnation; when he was rich, for our sakes becoming poor – taking part of flesh and blood, because we partook of the same; being made of a woman, that for us he might be made under the law, even for our sakes.

Lovely in the whole *course* of his life, and the more than angelical holiness and obedience which, in the depth of poverty and persecution, he exercised therein – doing good, receiving evil; blessing, and being cursed, reviled, reproached, all his days.

Lovely in his *death*; yea, therein most lovely to sinners – never more glorious and desirable than when he came broken, dead, from the cross. Then had he carried all our sins into a land of forgetfulness; then had he made peace and reconciliation for us; then had he procured life and immortality for us.

Lovely in his whole *employment*, in his great undertaking – in his *life*, *death*, *resurrection*, *ascension*; being a mediator between God and us, to recover the glory of God's justice, and to save our souls – to bring us to an enjoyment of God, who were set at such an infinite distance from him by sin.

Lovely in the glory and majesty wherewith he is *crowned*. Now he is set down at the right hand of the Majesty on high; where, though he be terrible to his enemies, yet he is full of mercy, love, and compassion, towards his beloved ones.

Lovely in all those *supplies of grace and consolations*, in all the dispensations of his Holy Spirit, whereof his saints are made partakers.

Lovely in all the *tender care, power, and wisdom*, which he exercises in the protection, safe-guarding, and delivery of his church and people, in the midst of all the oppositions and persecutions whereunto they are exposed.

Lovely in all his *ordinances*, and the whole of that spiritually glorious worship which he hath appointed to his people, whereby they draw nigh and have communion with him and his Father.

Lovely and glorious in the *vengeance* he taketh, and will finally execute, upon the stubborn enemies of himself and his people.

Lovely in the *pardon* he hath purchased and doth dispense, in the reconciliation he hath established, in the grace he communicates, in the consolations he doth administer, in the peace and joy he gives his saints, in his assured preservation of them unto glory.

What shall I say? There is no end of his excellencies and desirableness. 'He is altogether lovely. This is our beloved, and this is our friend, O daughters of Jerusalem.' "

Let our final word be just this. Having sought to consider something of heaven as a whole, and having ended on this high note of the Lamb being the focus of heaven, well may we ask ourselves: if the Lord Jesus Christ is so lovely to his own while he is in heaven and we are upon the earth, how lovely will he appear when we see the King in his beauty, when we are actually with Christ, and when we are made like him?

References

1 Richard Brooks, *The Lamb is All the Glory*, Evangelical Press
2 James Beverlin Ramsey, *Revelation*, Banner of Truth, p270
3 Preface to *Farewell Sermons*, Soli Deo Gloria, pv
4 Gordon H Clark, in his Foreword to Stephen Charnock's *The Existence and Attributes of God*, Sovereign Grace Publishers, p5
5 J C Ryle, *The True Christian*, Evangelical Press, p280. This volume was originally published as *The Christian Race*. The extended quotation at the end of chapter 4 is from this book
6 Ramsey, *Revelation*, p327
7 Quoted in Faith Cook, *Singing in the Fire*, Banner of Truth, p116
8 Philip Edgcumbe Hughes, *The Book of the Revelation*, IVP, p99
9 Brooks, *The Lamb is All the Glory*, p86
10 C H Spurgeon, *Metropolitan Tabernacle Pulpit*, volume 30, Banner of Truth, p507. Further Spurgeon references in this chapter are from this same sermon. Pilgrim Publications have republished all the volumes of Spurgeon's sermons.
11 Lachlan Mackenzie, *The Happy Man*, Banner of Truth, p87
12 Thomas Brooks, *Works*, volume 1, Banner of Truth, p418. The later reference to Brooks in this chapter is from p422.
13 Charles Ross, *The Inner Sanctuary*, Banner of Truth, p243f
14 Thomas Watson, *The Beatitudes,* Banner of Truth, p198
15 From p1220 of an aged commentary I have by William Burkitt on the New Testament. His dates were 1650-1703
16 Herman Hoeksema, *Behold He Cometh*, Reformed Free Publishing Association, p500f
17 From *Memoir and Remains of Robert Murray M'Cheyne*, by Andrew A Bonar, Banner of Truth, p499f
18 J C Ryle, *The Upper Room*, Banner of Truth, p91f
19 Ramsey, *Revelation*, p208
20 Geoffrey B Wilson, *Revelation*, Evangelical Press, p44
21 Ramsey, *Revelation*, p214
22 Hoeksema, *Behold He Cometh*, p148
23 A W Pink, *Comfort for Christians*, Baker, p81
24 Ryle, *The True Christian*, p261
25 Taken from *Thomas Charles' Spiritual Counsels*, Banner of Truth, p82ff.

26 Spurgeon, *Metropolitan Tabernacle Pulpit*, volume 35, p398. Further Spurgeon references in this chapter are from this same sermon.

27 R M M'Cheyne, *A Basket of Fragments*, Christian Focus Publications, p162ff.

28 Donald MacDonald, *Christian Experience*, Banner of Truth, p129

29 MacDonald, *Christian Experience*, p130f

30 *Letters of Samuel Rutherford*, Banner of Truth. See also, from the same publisher, Faith Cook's two books, *Grace in Winter* and *Samuel Rutherford and his Friends*.

31 See John Blanchard, *Whatever Happened to Hell?*, Evangelical Press.

32 William Hendriksen, *More Than Conquerors*, on p120 in my old Tyndale Press edition

33 Paul Helm, *The Last Things*, Banner of Truth, p112f. See the whole of his chapter 5 in particular, including the two following remarks. 'For hell is not a place of corruption, a diabolical society, a community out of God's reach. It is where corruption is impeccably punished, punished according to strict justice. In this sense God reigns in hell as he reigns in heaven' (p112). 'Heaven is founded upon the justice of God in accepting Christ's righteousness on behalf of sinners; hell is founded on the justice of God in punishing sinners' (p115)

34 Thomas Boston, *Human Nature in its Fourfold State*, Banner of Truth. Note especially, in the present connection, section IV on the eternal state.

35 See, for example, Ralph Robinson, *Christ All and in All*, Soli Deo Gloria

36 Spurgeon, *Metropolitan Tabernacle Pulpit*, volume 35, p387 and p390

37 MacDonald, *Christian Experience*, p135

38 *The Works of John Owen* are published by the Banner of Truth, as are the works of Thomas Brooks, Jonathan Edwards and John Bunyan, from which also I have quoted extensively. For the Richard Baxter material at the end of chapter 5 I used a 1978 Evangelical Press edition of his treatise.